The Zapatista Social Netwar in Mexico

DAVID RONFELDT · JOHN ARQUILLA · GRAHAM E. FULLER · MELISSA FULLER

D1715107

Prepared for the United States Army

RAND
ArroyoCenter

RAND

For more information on the RAND Arroyo Center, contact the Director of Operations, (310) 393-0411, extension 6500, or visit the Arroyo Center's Web site at http://www.rand.org/organization/ard/

This study was prepared for a research project on "Stability and the Military in Mexico." The research was sponsored by Deputy Chief of Staff for Intelligence and was conducted in RAND Arroyo Center's Strategy and Doctrine Program. The Arroyo Center is a federally funded research and development center sponsored by the United States Army.

The study reports on a case of "netwar," a concept that we have been developing for the purpose of understanding the nature of conflict in the information age (Arquilla and Ronfeldt, 1996b). Although the focus is on the Zapatista movement in Mexico, and on the responses thereto of the Mexican government and army, the study also identifies some implications for possible future netwars elsewhere around the world.

This study focuses mainly on the 1994–1996 period, in part because that was the heyday of this social netwar, but also because the study's preliminary findings were initially briefed to the sponsor in June 1996, and the first draft appeared in December 1996. This final publication is much revised and updated from the draft.

Please direct comments to:

David Ronfeldt
International Studies Group
RAND
Santa Monica, CA 90407-2138
(310) 393-0411, extension 7717
ronfeldt@rand.org

John Arquilla
Interdisciplinary Academic Center
U.S. Naval Postgraduate School
Monterey, CA 93943
(408) 656-3450
jarquilla@nps.navy.mil

CONTENTS

FIGURES

TABLES

SUMMARY

The information revolution is leading to the rise of network forms of organization, whereby small, previously isolated groups can communicate, link up, and conduct coordinated joint actions as never before. This, in turn, is leading to a new mode of conflict—"netwar"—in which the protagonists depend on using network forms of organization, doctrine, strategy, and technology. Many actors across the spectrum of conflict—from terrorists, guerrillas, and criminals who pose security threats to social activists who do not—are developing netwar designs and capabilities.

The Zapatista movement in Mexico provides a seminal case of "social netwar." In January 1994, a guerrilla-like insurgency begun in Chiapas by the Zapatista National Liberation Army (EZLN), and the Mexican government's response to it, aroused a multitude of civil-society activists associated with a variety of nongovernmental organizations (NGOs) to "swarm"—electronically as well as physically—from the United States, Canada, and elsewhere into Mexico City and Chiapas. There, they linked up with Mexican NGOs to voice solidarity with the EZLN's demands and to press for nonviolent change. Thus, what began as a violent insurgency in an isolated region mutated into a nonviolent though no less disruptive "social netwar" that engaged activists from far and wide and had both national and foreign repercussions for Mexico.

This study examines the rise of this netwar, the information-age behaviors that characterize it (e.g., use of the Internet), its effects on the Mexican military, its implications for Mexico's stability, and its implications for the occurrence of social netwars elsewhere around the world in the future.

ACKNOWLEDGMENTS

We thank the other members of the project's overall research team—
Kevin McCarthy and Kevin O'Connell, along with Roderic Camp,
Caesar Sereseres, and Steve Wager—for ideas and observations they
provided. David Kassing, Tom McNaugher, Jim Quinlivan, and Tom
Szayna were additional sources of insight and advice at RAND's Ar-
royo Center.

Our thanks extend outside RAND to Armando Martínez, who worked
on an earlier version of this study (Ronfeldt and Martínez, 1996)
during a graduate-student summer internship at RAND in 1994; to
Sergio Aguayo, for comments he provided on that earlier version;
and to Paul de Armond and Joel Simon, because, although neither
was involved in this study, each has occasionally offered informative
and encouraging comments about the netwar concept. Our thanks
also extend to various Mexican and U.S. government officials and
social activists who provided illuminating comments during discussions and interviews. We particularly thank analysts in the Office of
the Army Deputy Chief of Staff for Intelligence for comments they
provided during and following an interim briefing about this study in
June 1996.

Turning the initial December 1996 draft of this study into this final,
much revised publication benefited greatly from comments received
from two outside reviewers: Deborah Avant (George Washington
University) and Donald Schulz (U.S. Army War College). We are
indebted to both of them for their counsel. Finally, we thank Nikki
Shacklett at RAND for her skillful editing of this study.

Chapter One

AN INSURGENCY BECOMES A SOCIAL NETWAR

Mexico's Zapatista movement exemplifies a new approach to social conflict that we call *social netwar*. Mexico, the nation that gave the world a prototype of social revolution early in the 20th century, has generated an information-age prototype of militant social netwar on the eve of the 21st century. This study examines the nature of this netwar and its implications, not only for Mexico but also for our understanding of the prospects for similar conflicts elsewhere.[1]

The insurrection by the Zapatista National Liberation Army (EZLN) erupted on New Year's Day 1994, when one to two thousand[2] variously armed insurgents occupied five towns and a city, San Cristóbal de las Casas, in the highlands of Mexico's southernmost state, Chiapas. Over the next few days, the EZLN declared war on the Mexican government, vowed to march on Mexico City, proclaimed a revolutionary agenda, began an international media campaign for sympathy and support, and invited foreign observers and monitors to come to Chiapas.

The Mexican government's initial reaction was quite traditional. It ordered army and police forces to suppress the insurrection and downplayed its size, scope, and causes, in keeping with official as-

---

[1]Although this report reflects new research, it should be noted that some of the text about Mexico and the Zapatista netwar is drawn, often verbatim, from writing that also appears in an earlier version (Ronfeldt and Martínez, 1996).

[2]The figures range from 500 to 4,000, depending on the source. The total number of troops plus support people available to the EZLN is sometimes said to run much higher, up to 12,000.

sertions a year earlier that no guerrillas existed in Chiapas. The rebels were characterized as "just 200 individuals with vague demands," and foreign influences from Guatemala and other parts of Central America were blamed. The government tried to project a picture of stability to the world, claiming this was an isolated, local outburst.

But during the few days that the EZLN held ground, it upstaged the government. Through star-quality spokesman "Subcomandante Marcos" in particular, the EZLN called a press conference and issued communiqués to disavow Marxist and other old ideological leanings. It denied it was tied to Central American guerrillas. It insisted its roots were indigenous, and that its demands were national in scope. It appealed for nationwide support for its agenda: respect for indigenous peoples; creation of a true democracy; and socioeconomic reforms, including, by implication, the abrogation of the North American Free Trade Agreement (NAFTA). At the same time, the EZLN denied it had a utopian blueprint or had figured out exactly how to resolve Mexico's problems. It also denied that it wanted to seize power. Meanwhile, the EZLN called on Mexican civil society— not other armed guerrillas, but peaceful activists—to join with it in a nationwide struggle for social, economic, and political change, without necessarily taking up arms. The EZLN also called on international organizations (notably, the Red Cross) and civil-society actors (notably, human-rights groups) to come to Chiapas to monitor the conflict. This was not at all a conventional way to mount an insurrection.

Against this background, the government mobilized the army, police, and other security forces. Within days, the number of army troops in Chiapas expanded from 2,000 to about 12,000. Air and ground attacks were conducted in rebel-held areas. Reports of casualties grew into the low hundreds. Reports also spread of human-rights abuses (including by EZLN forces).

As the EZLN withdrew into nearby rain forests and mountains, and ultimately into the lowlands of the Lacandón jungle up against the Mexico-Guatemala border, army and police units retook the towns and detained and interrogated people suspected of ties to the EZLN. Reports of tortures, executions, and disappearances at the hands of army and police units spread in the media. Meanwhile, government agents tried to prevent, or at least delay, some journalists and human-rights activists from entering the conflict zone; some were accused of meddling in Mexico's internal affairs. This heavy-handed response was not unusual; it reflected traditional practices in Mexico—as seen in the suppression of the student-led protest movement in 1968, in operations against urban terrorist and rural guerrilla movements in the 1970s, and in the occasional, less severe policing of violent electoral protests in the 1980s.[3]

The EZLN's media-savvy behavior and the Mexican government's heavy-handed response quickly aroused a multitude of foreign activists associated with human-rights, indigenous-rights, and other types of nongovernmental organizations (NGOs) to swarm—electronically as well as physically—out of the United States, Canada, and Europe into Mexico City and Chiapas. There, they linked with Mexican NGOs to voice sympathy and support for the EZLN's demands. They began to clamor nonviolently for the government to agree to a cease-fire, a military withdrawal, and negotiations with the EZLN. They also clamored for access to gather information and monitor conditions in the conflict zone. In the process, they made sure that the EZLN's agenda could not be kept local, and that global media held a focus on Chiapas. Furthermore, they added to calls for the Mexican government to undertake major democratic reforms. And then, on January 12, to everyone's surprise, Mexico's president agreed to enter negotiations and called a halt to combat operations.

This swarming by a large multitude of militant NGOs in response to a distant upheaval—the first major case anywhere—was no anomaly. It drew on two to three decades of relatively unnoticed organizational and technological changes around the world that meant the information revolution was altering the context and conduct of social conflict. Because of this, the NGOs were able to form into highly networked, loosely coordinated, cross-border coalitions to wage an information-age social netwar that would constrain the Mexican government and assist the EZLN's cause.

What began as a violent insurgency by a small indigenous force in an isolated region was thus transformed and expanded, within weeks,

---

[3]For background, see Wager and Schulz (1995) and Hellman (1988).

into a nonviolent, less overtly destructive, but still highly disruptive movement that engaged the involvement of activists from far and wide and had both foreign and national repercussions for Mexico. For the next two years, the activities of the Zapatista movement—especially the course of the EZLN's negotiations with the Mexican government—would dominate news headlines and stir wide-ranging debates about Mexico's future.   Indeed, in April 1995, after "information operations" had proved more significant than military combat operations for all sides, Foreign Minister Jose Angel Gurría would observe that

> Chiapas . . . is a place where there has not been a shot fired in the last fifteen months. . . . The shots lasted ten days, and ever since the war has been a war of ink, of written word, a war on the Internet.[4]

The netwar had its heyday in Mexico in 1994 and 1995. During 1996, negotiations between the government and the EZLN ground to a halt, the army confined the EZLN to a small zone in Chiapas, many social activists turned to focus on other issues, and the Zapatista movement receded as a matter of daily significance in Mexico, though it still aroused international attention by staging events like the First Intercontinental Encounter for Humanity and Against Neoliberalism. During 1997, the EZLN and its NGO allies had to make a major effort to remobilize as a movement and garner public attention to press the cause—as occurred with a march from Chiapas to Mexico City in September. Or else it took a dramatic resurgence of old-style violence in Chiapas—as happened when local pro-government paramilitary forces murdered numerous people, some of them Zapatista sympathizers, in the village of Acteal in December 1997—to remobilize the netwar's partisans and sympathizers in Mexico and abroad.

As of this writing (April 1998), the Zapatista social netwar (not to mention the EZLN's capacity for insurgency) is seemingly past its peak, though it has not ended or lost all prospect for reactivation. Whatever comes next—possibly a peaceful settlement if the govern-

---

[4]From a speech by Gurría before businessmen from 37 countries, as reported by Rodolfo Montes, "Chiapas Is a War of Ink and Internet," *Reforma*, April 26, 1995, translation, as circulated on the Internet.

ment demonstrates renewed interest in negotiations, or, at the other extreme, possibly a violent return to insurgency involving more than the EZLN on the eve of the year 2000 elections—the Zapatista netwar has already had profound effects, and not just in Mexico. It has shaken the foundations of the Mexican political system, by creating extraordinary pressure for democratic reforms and raising the specter of instability in America's next-door neighbor. More to the point, it is inspiring radical activists around the world to begin thinking that old models of struggle—ones that call for building "parties" and "fronts" and *"focos"* to "crush the state" and "seize power"—are not the way to go in the information age. A new concept, akin to the Zapatista movement, is emerging that aims to draw on the power of "networks" and strengthen "global civil society" in order to counterbalance state and market actors.

The next chapter provides an overview of the concept and practice of netwar. We discuss the rise of network forms of organization and the implications for conflict in the information age. We also identify some propositions about networks-versus-hierarchies that apply to the development of *counternetwar.*

In the subsequent chapters, the Zapatista movement is analyzed from this netwar perspective. We inquire into the causes of the conflict, the nature of the protagonists and their allies, and the conduct of the netwar, with an emphasis on the Zapatistas' information operations.

The final chapters discuss this social netwar's effects in Mexico, including the diffusion of unrest to other parts of the country, as exemplified by the appearance of the Popular Revolutionary Army (EPR). We also identify some implications for anticipating new social netwars beyond the Mexican case.

Chapter Two

THE ADVENT OF NETWAR: ANALYTIC BACKGROUND

The information revolution is altering the nature of conflict across the spectrum. There are many reasons for this, but we would call attention to two in particular.[1]

First, the information revolution is favoring and strengthening network forms of organization, while simultaneously making life difficult for old hierarchical forms. The rise of networks—especially "all-channel" networks, in which every node is connected to every other node—means that power is migrating to nonstate actors, who are able to organize into sprawling multiorganizational networks more readily than traditional, hierarchical, state actors can. This means that conflicts will increasingly be waged by "networks," perhaps more than by "hierarchies." It also means that whoever masters the network form stands to gain major advantages.

Second, as the information revolution deepens, conflicts increasingly depend on information and communications matters. More than ever before, conflicts are about "knowledge"—about who knows (or can be kept from knowing) what, when, where, and why. Conflicts will revolve less around the use of raw power than of "soft power" (Nye, 1990; Nye and Owens, 1996), as applied through "information operations" and "perception management"—that is, media-oriented measures that aim to attract rather than coerce and that affect how

---

[1]While all the co-authors contributed to this chapter, the analytical background is mostly drawn, often verbatim, from Arquilla and Ronfeldt (1996b). For additional discussion of new views of "information" and "power," see Arquilla and Ronfeldt (1996a). Also see Toffler and Toffler (1993).

secure a society, a military, or other actor feels about its knowledge of itself and its adversaries. Psychosocial disruption may become more important than physical destruction.

These propositions cut cross the entire conflict spectrum. Major transformations are thus looming in the nature of adversaries, in the kinds of threats they may pose, and in how conflicts can be waged. Information-age threats are likely to be more diffuse, dispersed, nonlinear, multidimensional, and ambiguous than industrial-age threats. Metaphorically, future conflicts may resemble the Eastern game of go more than the Western game of chess.

As a result, the information-age conflict spectrum increasingly looks like this:

- *Cyberwar*—a concept that refers to information-oriented military warfare (Arquilla and Ronfeldt, 1993, 1997)[2]—is becoming an important entry at the military end of the spectrum, where the language is normally about high-intensity conflicts (HICs) and middle-range conflicts (MRCs).[3]

- *Netwar* (Arquilla and Ronfeldt, 1996b, 1997) figures increasingly at the societal end of the spectrum, where the language is normally about small-scale contingencies (SSCs)—recently known as low-intensity conflict (LIC) and operations other than war (OOTW)—and nonmilitary modes of conflict (and crime).

---

[2]The term *cyberwar* is taking on a life of its own. Arquilla and Ronfeldt (1993) offer the original definition, followed by a more refined one (1997), reflecting a broad perspective as to how the information revolution implies the redesign of military organization, doctrine, and strategy. A cover story in *Time* magazine in 1995 and the book by Campen, Dearth, and Goodden (1996) reflect the original definition, but give it a high-tech flavor. Continuing this trend, Molander, Riddile, and Wilson (1996) narrow it to a synonym for "strategic information warfare" (SIW), mainly meaning attacks on computerized infrastructures for information and communications. But in our view, cyberwar may or may not involve SIW—and it may involve a lot more than SIW. The effort to reduce cyberwar to a high-tech activity neglects the broader dimensions of military organization, doctrine, and strategy, and the ways that they gain importance in the information age. As discussed later, a reductionist view is also affecting the term *netwar*, where it is taken to refer only to war on the Internet—another mistake, in our view.

[3]MRC is also used to refer to major regional conflict. That term is now giving way to major theater war (MTW).

Whereas cyberwar usually pits formal military forces against each other, netwar is more likely to involve nonstate, paramilitary, and irregular forces. Both concepts are consistent with the views of analysts like Martin Van Creveld (1991) who believe that a "transformation of war" is under way. Neither concept is simply about technology; both refer to *comprehensive* approaches to conflict based on the centrality of information—comprehensive in that they combine organizational, doctrinal, strategic, tactical, and technological innovations, for offense and defense.

DEFINITION OF NETWAR

To be more precise, the term *netwar* refers to an emerging mode of conflict (and crime) at societal levels, involving measures short of traditional war, in which the protagonists use network forms of organization and related doctrines, strategies, and technologies attuned to the information age. These protagonists are likely to consist of dispersed small groups who communicate, coordinate, and conduct their campaigns in an internetted manner, without a precise central command. Thus, netwar differs from modes of conflict and crime in which the protagonists prefer hierarchical organizations, doctrines, and strategies, as in past efforts to build, for example, centralized movements along Leninist lines. Netwar is about the Middle East's Hamas more than the Palestine Liberation Organization (PLO), Mexico's Zapatistas more than Cuba's Fidelistas, and America's Christian Patriot movement more than the Ku Klux Klan.[4] It is also about the Asian Triads more than the Sicilian Mafia, and Chicago's "Gangsta Disciples" more than the Al Capone Gang.

The term is meant to call attention to the prospect that network-based conflict and crime will become major phenomena in the decades ahead. Various actors across the spectrum of conflict and crime are already evolving in the direction of netwar. This includes familiar adversaries who are modifying their structures and strategies to take advantage of networked designs: e.g., transnational terrorist

---

[4]This is just a short exemplary statement. Many other examples could be noted. Instead of Hamas, for example, we might have mentioned the Committee for the Legitimate Defense of Human Rights (CLDHR), an anti-Saudi organization based in London.

groups, black-market proliferators of weapons of mass destruction (WMD), drug and other crime syndicates, fundamentalist and ethno-nationalist movements, intellectual-property pirates, and immigration and refugee smugglers. Some urban gangs, rural militia organizations, and militant single-issue groups in the United States are also developing netwar-like attributes. The netwar spectrum also includes a new generation of revolutionaries, radicals, and activists who are just beginning to create information-age ideologies, in which identities and loyalties may shift from the nation-state to the transnational level of "global civil society." New kinds of actors, such as anarchistic and nihilistic leagues of computer-hacking "cyboteurs," may also partake of netwar.

Many if not most netwar actors will be nonstate, even stateless. Some may be agents of a state, but others may try to turn states into *their* agents. Moreover, a netwar actor may be both subnational and transnational in scope. Odd hybrids and symbioses are likely. Furthermore, some actors (e.g., violent terrorist and criminal organizations) may threaten U.S. and other nations' interests, but other actors (e.g., peaceful NGO activists) may not. Some actors may aim at destruction, but more may aim mainly at disruption. Again, many variations are possible.

The full spectrum of netwar proponents may thus seem broad and odd at first glance. But there is an underlying pattern that cuts across all variations: the use of *network forms of organization, doctrine, strategy, and technology attuned to the information age.*

Caveats About the Role of Technology

Netwar is a result of the rise of network forms of organization, which in turn is a result of the computerized information revolution.[5] To realize its potential, any kind of fully interconnected network requires a capacity for constant, dense information and communications flows, more so than do other forms of organization (e.g., hierarchies). This is afforded by the latest information and communication technologies—cellular telephones, fax machines, electronic mail

---

[5]For explanation of this point, see Ronfeldt (1996) and Arquilla and Ronfeldt (1996b), not to mention other sources cited in those documents.

(e-mail), World Wide Web (WWW) sites, and computer conferencing. Such technologies are highly advantageous for a netwar actor.

But a couple of caveats are in order. First, the new technologies, however enabling for organizational networking, may not be the only crucial technologies for a netwar actor. Old technologies, like human couriers, and mixes of old and new systems may, in some situations, do the job.

Second, netwar is not simply a function of "the Net" (i.e., the Internet); it does not take place only in "cyberspace" or the "infosphere." Some key *battles* may occur there, but a *war's* overall conduct and outcome will normally depend mostly on what happens in the "real world"—and this will continue to be, even in information-age conflicts, generally more important than what happens in cyberspace or the infosphere.[6]

Efforts to reduce the netwar concept to being just about Internet-war should be guarded against, along with other efforts to reduce the cyberwar concept to being just about "strategic information warfare." Americans have a tendency to view modern conflict as being more about technology than organization and doctrine. In our view, this is a misleading if not error-prone tendency.[7]

More About Organizational Design

In an archetypal netwar, the protagonists are likely to amount to a set of diverse, dispersed "nodes" who share a set of ideas and interests and who are arrayed to act in a fully internetted "all-channel" manner. As the scholarly literature instructs (e.g., Evan, 1972), networks come in basically three types (or topologies):

---

[6]Paul Kneisel, "Netwar: The Battle Over Rec.Music.White-Power," *ANTIFA INFO-BULLETIN*, Research Supplement, June 12, 1996; unpaginated ascii text available on the Internet. He analyzes the largest vote ever taken about the creation of a new Usenet newsgroup—a vote to prevent the creation of a group that was ostensibly about white-power music. He concludes that "The war against contemporary fascism will be won in the 'real world' off the net; but battles against fascist netwar are fought and won on the Internet." His title is testimony to the spreading usage of the term *netwar*.

[7]See footnote 2, and Arquilla and Ronfeldt (1997, ch. 1).

- the *chain* network, as in a migration or smuggling chain where people, goods, or information move along a line of separated contacts, and where end-to-end communication must travel through the intermediate nodes;

- the *star*, hub, or wheel network, as in a franchise or a cartel structure where a set of actors are tied to a central (but not hierarchical) node or actor, and must go through that node to communicate and coordinate with each other;

- the *all-channel* network, as in a collaborative network of militant peace groups where everybody is connected to everybody else.

See Figure 1. Each node indicated in the diagrams may refer to an individual, a group, an institution, part of a group or institution, or even a state. The nodes may be large or small, tightly or loosely coupled, and inclusive or exclusive in membership. They may be segmentary or specialized—that is, they may look alike and engage in similar activities, or they may undertake a division of labor based on specialization. The boundaries of the network may be well defined, or they may be blurred and porous in relation to the outside environment.

Each design is suited to different conditions and purposes, and all three may be found among netwar-related adversaries: e.g., the chain in smuggling operations; the star among criminal syndicates;

RAND *MR994.1*

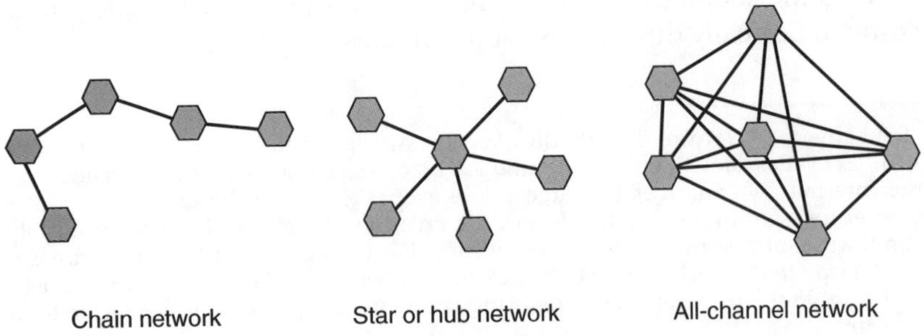

Chain network   Star or hub network   All-channel network

Figure 1—Types of Networks

and the all-channel among militant groups that are highly internet-ted and decentralized. There may also be hybrids of the three types, with different tasks being organized around different types of networks. For example, a netwar actor may have an all-channel council or directorate at its core but use stars and chains for tactical operations. There may also be hybrids of network and hierarchical forms of organization. For example, traditional hierarchies may exist inside particular nodes in a network. Some actors may have a hierarchical organization overall but use network designs for tactical operations; other actors may have an all-channel network design overall but use hierarchical teams for tactical operations. Many combinations and configurations are possible.

Of the three, the all-channel type has been the most difficult to organize and sustain, partly because of the dense communications it may require. But it is the type that gives the network form its new, high potential for collaborative undertakings. It is the type that is gaining new strength from the information revolution. And it is the type that we generally refer to in this study—and in the remainder of this chapter.

Pictorially, then, such a netwar actor resembles a geodesic "Bucky ball" (named for Buckminster Fuller); it does not look like a pyramid.[8] The organizational design is flat. Ideally, there is no single, central leadership, command, or headquarters—no precise heart or head that can be targeted. The network as a whole (but not necessarily each node) has little to no hierarchy; there may be multiple leaders. Decisionmaking and operations are decentralized, allowing for local initiative and autonomy. Thus the design may look acephalous (headless) at times, and polycephalous (Hydra-headed) at other times, though not all nodes may be "created equal." In other words, it is a heterarchy, or what may be better termed a "panarchy."

The capacity of this design for effective performance over time may depend on the existence of shared principles, interests, and goals— perhaps an overarching doctrine or ideology—which spans all nodes and to which the members subscribe in a deep way. Such a set of

---

[8]The structure may also be cellular. However, the presence of "cells" does not necessarily mean a network exists. A hierarchy can also be cellular, as is the case with some subversive organizations.

principles, shaped through mutual consultation and consensus building, can enable them to be "all of one mind" even though they are dispersed and devoted to different tasks. It can provide a central ideational, strategic, and operational coherence that allows for tactical decentralization. It can set boundaries and provide guidelines for decisions and actions so that the members do not have to resort to a hierarchy—"they know what they have to do."[9]

The design depends on the network having a capacity—indeed, a well-developed infrastructure—for the dense communication of functional information. This does not mean that all nodes must be in constant communication; that may not make sense for a secretive, conspiratorial actor. But when communication is needed, the network's members must be able to disseminate information promptly and as broadly as desired within the network and to outside audiences.

In many respects, then, the archetypal netwar design corresponds to what earlier analysts (Gerlach (1987), p. 115, based on Gerlach and Hine (1970)) called a "segmented, polycentric, ideologically integrated network" (SPIN):

> By segmentary I mean that it is cellular, composed of many different groups. . . . By polycentric I mean that it has many different leaders or centers of direction. . . . By networked I mean that the segments and the leaders are integrated into reticulated systems or networks through various structural, personal, and ideological ties. Networks are usually unbounded and expanding. . . . This acronym [SPIN] helps us picture this organization as a fluid, dynamic, expanding one, spinning out into mainstream society.[10]

---

[9]The phrase in quotation marks reflects a doctrinal statement by Beam (1992) about "Leaderless Resistance," which has strongly influenced right-wing white-power groups.

[10]This SPIN concept is a precursor of the netwar concept. Proposed by Luther Gerlach and Virginia Hine in the 1960s to depict U.S. social movements, it anticipates many points about network forms of organization that are now coming into focus in the analysis of not only social movements but also some terrorist, criminal, ethnonationalist, and fundamentalist organizations.

Swarming, and the Blurring of Offense and Defense

This distinctive, often ad hoc design has unusual strengths, for both offense and defense. On the offense, networks are known for being adaptable, flexible, and versatile vis-à-vis opportunities and challenges. This may be particularly the case where a set of actors can engage in *swarming*. Little analytic attention has been given to swarming, yet it may become the key mode of conflict in the information age, and the cutting edge for this possibility is found among netwar protagonists.[11]

Swarming occurs when the dispersed nodes of a network of small (and perhaps some large) forces can converge on a target from multiple directions. The overall aim is *sustainable pulsing*—swarm networks must be able to coalesce rapidly and stealthily on a target, then dissever and redisperse, immediately ready to recombine for a new pulse. The capacity for a "stealthy approach" suggests that, in netwar, attacks are more likely to occur in "swarms" than in more traditional "waves."

Swarming may be most effective, and difficult to defend against, where a set of netwar actors do not have to "mass" their forces but can engage in "packetization" (for want of a better term). This means, for example, that drug smugglers can break large loads into many small packets for simultaneous surreptitious transport across a border, or that NGO activists, as in the case of the Zapatista movement, have enough diversity in their ranks to go after any discrete issue area that arises—human rights, democracy, the environment, rural development, and so forth.

In terms of defensive potential, networks tend to be redundant and diverse, making them robust and resilient in the face of adversity. Where they have a capacity for interoperability and shun centralized command and control, network designs can be difficult to crack and defeat as a whole. In particular, they may defy counterleadership targeting. This limits whoever would attack a network—generally, they can find and confront only portions of it. Moreover, the deniability built into a network affords the possibility that it may simply

---

[11]Swarm networks, and the capacity of networks for swarming, are raised by Kelly (1994). For recent thinking about swarming, see Arquilla and Ronfeldt (1997).

absorb a number of attacks on distributed nodes, leading the attacker to believe the network has been harmed when, in fact, it remains viable, and is seeking new opportunities for tactical surprise.

The difficulty of dealing with netwar actors is deepened when the lines between offense and defense are blurred or blended. When *blurring* is the case, it may be difficult to distinguish between attacking and defending actions, particularly where an actor goes on the offense in the name of self-defense. As we shall discuss, the Zapatista struggle in Mexico demonstrates anew the blurring of offense and defense. The *blending* of offense and defense will often mix the strategic and tactical levels of operations. For example, where guerrillas are on the defensive strategically, they may go on the offense tactically; the war of the *mujahideen* in Afghanistan provides a modern example.

Operating in the Cracks

The blurring of offense and defense reflects another feature of netwar: It tends to defy and cut across standard boundaries, jurisdictions, and distinctions between state and society, public and private, war and peace, war and crime, civilian and military, police and military, and legal and illegal. This makes it difficult if not nigh impossible for a government to assign to a single agency—e.g., military, police, or intelligence—the responsibility for responding.

As Colonel Richard Szafranski (1994, 1995) illuminates in discussing how information warfare ultimately becomes "neo-cortical warfare," the challenge for governments and societies becomes "epistemological." A netwar actor may aim to confound people's fundamental beliefs about the nature of their culture, society, and government, partly to foment fear but perhaps mainly to disorient people and unhinge their perceptions. This is why social netwar tends to be about disruption more than destruction. The more epistemological the challenge, the more confounding it may be from an organizational standpoint. Whose responsibility is it to respond? Whose roles and missions are at stake? Is it a military, police, intelligence, or political matter? When the roles and missions of defenders are not easy to define, both deterrence and defense may become quite problematic.

Thus, the spread of netwar adds to the challenges facing the nation-state in the information age. Traditionally, ideals of sovereignty and authority are linked to a bureaucratic rationality in which issues and problems can be sliced up, and specific offices can be charged with taking care of specific problems. In netwar, things are rarely so clear. A protagonist is likely to operate in the cracks and gray areas of a society, striking where lines of authority crisscross and the operational paradigms of politicians, officials, soldiers, police officers, and related actors get fuzzy and clash. Moreover, where transnational participation is strong, a netwar's protagonists may expose a local government to challenges to its sovereignty and legitimacy, by arousing foreign governments and business corporations to put pressure on the local government to alter its domestic policies and practices.

NETWORKS VERSUS HIERARCHIES: CHALLENGES FOR COUNTERNETWAR

Against this background, the emerging theory and practice of netwar involves a set of general propositions about the information revolution and its implications for netwar and *counternetwar* (Arquilla and Ronfeldt, 1993, 1996b):[12]

Hierarchies have a difficult time fighting networks. Examples of this exist across the conflict spectrum. Some of the best are found in the failings of many governments to defeat transnational criminal cartels engaged in drug smuggling, as in Colombia. The persistence of religious revivalist movements, as in Algeria, in the face of unremitting state opposition, shows the robustness of the network form on defense and offense. The Zapatista movement in Mexico, with its legions of supporters and sympathizers among local and transnational NGOs, shows that social netwar can put a democratizing autocracy on the defensive and pressure it to continue adopting reforms.

It takes networks to fight networks. Governments that would defend against netwar will, increasingly, have to adopt organizational designs and strategies like those of their adversaries. This does not

---

[12]Also see Berger (1998) for additional thinking and analysis about such propositions.

mean mirroring the adversary, but rather learning to draw on the same design principles that he has already learned about the rise of network forms in the information age. These principles depend to some extent upon technological innovation, but mainly on a willingness to innovate organizationally and doctrinally, perhaps especially by building new mechanisms for interagency and multijurisdictional cooperation.

Whoever masters the network form first and best will gain major advantages. In these early decades of the information age, adversaries who have advanced at networking (be they criminals, terrorists, or peaceful social activists) are enjoying an increase in their power relative to state agencies. While networking once allowed them simply to keep from being suppressed, it now allows them to compete on more nearly equal terms with states and other hierarchically oriented actors. The histories of Hamas and the Cali cartel illustrate this; so does the Zapatista movement in Mexico.

An implication for governments is that counternetwar may require very effective interagency approaches, which by their nature involve networked structures. It is not necessary, desirable, or even possible to replace all hierarchies with networks in governments. Rather, where relevant, the challenge will be to blend these two forms skillfully while retaining enough core authority to encourage and enforce adherence to networked processes. By creating effective hybrids, governments may become better prepared to confront the new threats and challenges emerging in the information age, whether generated by terrorists, militias, criminals, or other actors. (For elaboration, see Arquilla and Ronfeldt (1997), ch. 19.)

VARIETIES OF NETWAR

Netwar is a deduced concept—it derives from our thinking about the effects and implications of the information revolution. Once coined, the concept has helped us see that evidence is mounting about the rise of network forms of organization, and about the importance of "information strategies" and "information operations" across the spectrum of conflict, including among terrorists, guerrillas, criminals, and activists.[13] In noting this, we are not equating terrorists, guerrillas, criminals, or activists with each other—each has different dynamics. Nor do we mean to tarnish social activism, which has many positive aspects for civil society.[14] We are simply calling attention to a cross-cutting meta-pattern about network forms of organization, doctrine, and strategy that we might not have spotted, by induction or deduction, if we had been experts focused solely on any one of those areas.

Terrorist and Criminal Netwar

Terrorism continues to evolve in the direction of violent netwar (see Arquilla, Ronfeldt, and Zanini, forthcoming). Islamic fundamentalist organizations like Hamas, as well as right-wing militias and extremist groups in the United States that rely on a doctrine of "leaderless resistance" propounded by Aryan nationalist Louis Beam (Beam, 1992; Stern, 1996), consist of groups organized in loosely interconnected, semi-independent cells that have no single commanding hierarchy above them.[15] Hamas exemplifies the shift away from a hierarchically oriented movement based on a "great leader" (like the PLO and Yassir Arafat). Instead, Hamas is characterized by "a loose network of cells without a strict hierarchy or central base." As Israeli General David Agmon has noted, "Hamas is not one organization, but many [which are] connected in a sort of network to other such groups."[16] More to the point, Hamas's organization is "cellular; very loosely structured, with some elements working openly through mosques and social service institutions to recruit members, raise money, organize activities, and distribute propaganda; other elements operate clandestinely, advocating and using violence" (Builta, 1996, pp. 776,

---

[13]These are not the only types of netwar actors; there are others. For example, corporations may also engage in netwars.

[14]See the discussion in Ronfeldt (1996).

[15]The *New York Times* and *Los Angeles Times* insightfully covered this trend among Islamic fundamentalist groups in 1996. See John Kifner, "Alms and Arms: Tactics in a Holy War," *The New York Times*, Friday, March 15, 1996, pp. A-1, A-6, A-7; and John-Thor Dahlburg, "Technology Lets Tentacles of Terrorism Extend Reach," *Los Angeles Times*, Tuesday, August 6, 1996, pp. A-1, A-10, A-11.

[16]Material quoted from Nicolas B. Tatro, "Loose Structure Helps Make Hamas Elusive," *Associated Press*, March 13, 1996.

781). Also, Hamas has numerous "network contacts" to other terrorist groups (e.g., Hizbollah, al-Nahda, Muslim Brotherhood), to non-state organizations like the U.S. Nation of Islam, and to states (e.g., Iran, Syria).

As for criminal netwar, transnational criminal organizations (TCOs) are gaining strength around the world largely because they are so adept at building networks to take advantage of global interconnections (Sterling, 1994; Williams, 1994). Phil Williams describes these TCOs in words that could also apply to terrorist organizations:

> TCOs are diverse in structure, outlook and membership. What they have in common is that they are highly mobile and adaptable and are able to operate across national borders with great ease. . . . They are able to do this partly because of the conditions identified above and partly because of their emphasis on networks rather than formal organizations. (Williams, 1994, p. 105.)

Social Netwar

Analytically, much the same may be said about social netwar, the focus of this study. Militant social activists, even though their purposes, strategies, and tactics are far removed from those of terrorists and criminals, are increasingly organized into transnational "issue-networks." According to Kathryn Sikkink's work on the rise of human-rights networks:

> An international issue-network comprises a set of organizations, bound by shared values and by dense exchanges of information and services, working internationally on an issue. . . . [I]nternational and domestic NGOs play a central role in all issue-networks. They are the most proactive members of the networks, usually initiating actions and pressuring more powerful actors to take positions. . . . As a result of this exchange of information and services, of flows of funds, and of shared norms and goals, the members of the issue-network work together in a constant but informal, uncoordinated, and nonhierarchical manner. (Sikkink, 1993, pp. 415–417.)

As for doctrine and strategy, human-rights issue-networks operate "by changing the information environment in which state actors work" (Sikkink, 1993, p. 441). While NGO activists may want to shape the information environment in a distant conflict zone and in the offices of the local government, it may be even more important for them to affect the information environment abroad, notably in Washington, D.C., and in the global media.[17] As Sikkink (1993, pp. 439–440) clarifies, modern issue-networks differ, to some degree, from traditional grass-roots and social movements; issue-networks may have associates, such as international organizations and philanthropic foundations, that are not normally found as part of those traditional movements.[18]

The rise of energetic social netwarriors may thus transform the nature of "strategic public diplomacy." It is traditionally concerned with the interactions of states, as they attempt to manipulate media in pursuit of their foreign policy goals (Manheim, 1994). Now, however, the initiative seems to be shifting to nonstate actors, as they are gaining comparable access to media, are less vulnerable to "targeting" themselves, and, in general, pursue agendas that are more suited to information-oriented issues of equity and human rights as opposed to the *realpolitik*-driven policies of nation-states.

In sum, then, social netwar is characterized by militant activists operating in, and as, SPINs or issue-networks. Social netwars tend to be anti-establishment, but any particular one may be progressive or reactionary, left- or right-wing, mass or sectarian, public or covert, threatening or promising for a society—it all depends. Whatever the case, networks of activist NGOs challenge a government (or rival NGOs) in a public issue area, and the "war" is mainly over "information"—who knows what, when, where, and why. Social netwar aims to affect what an opponent knows, or thinks it knows, not only about a challenger but also about itself and the world around it. More broadly, social netwar aims to shape beliefs and attitudes in the surrounding social milieu. A social netwar is likely to in-

---

[17]These kinds of analytical points by Sikkink and other researchers (e.g., Gerlach, 1987; Thorup, 1991) have finally begun to filter into the writings of policymakers. See Mathews (1997) and Slaughter (1997). For additional citations see Ronfeldt (1996).

[18]There is a definitional gray area here. Some grass-roots movements and social movements, especially what are called "new social movements," are close to being issue-networks, and some may have netwar-like characteristics and capabilities. The point still stands, however, that the literature about grass-roots movements and social movements has been slow to emphasize the rise of network forms of organization, doctrine, strategy, and technology.

volve battles for public opinion and for media access and coverage, at local through global levels. It is also likely to revolve around propaganda campaigns, psychological warfare, and strategic public diplomacy, not just to educate and inform, but to deceive and disinform as well. It resembles a nonmilitary version of "neo-cortical warfare" (Szafranski, 1994, 1995).

In other words, social netwar is more about a doctrinal leader like Subcomandante Marcos than about a lone, wild computer hacker like Kevin Mitnick.

MEXICO—SCENE OF MULTIPLE NETWARS

Mexico is currently the scene of multiple netwars that challenge the stability and the reformability of the Mexican system. For example, the Popular Revolutionary Army (EPR) aims to wage terrorist/ guerrilla netwar. It is not entirely clear that the EPR qualifies well as an armed netwar actor, since its design remains obscure to analysis, but it has netwar-like characteristics that we discuss later. As for criminal netwar, Mexico's internetted drug-trafficking cartels are the key culprits. They have evolved aggressively in this direction since the late 1980s, partly in league with Colombian cartels.

The world's leading example of social netwar lies in the decentralized, dispersed cooperation among the myriad Mexican and transnational activist NGOs that support or sympathize with the EZLN and that aim to affect Mexico's policies on human rights, democracy, and other reform issues. That is the subject of this study. Indeed, the points made above about social netwar apply well to the Zapatista movement. It involves myriad issue-networks—for human rights, indigenous rights, etc.—that operate in a nonhierarchical fashion and through shifting coalitions and ad hoc formations. And the Zapatista movement's networks are indeed held together by shared values, dense exchanges of information, and efforts to mount "information operations" against the Mexican government and other actors that the network aims to influence.

Chapter Three

EMERGENCE OF THE ZAPATISTA NETWAR

The EZLN's Zapatistas are rural insurgents. But they are not ordinary ones, and they were quickly perceived by intellectuals (e.g., Mexico's Carlos Fuentes, Pablo Gonzalez Casanova) as representing the world's first postcommunist, "postmodern" insurgency:

> Many people with cloudy minds in Mexico responded to what happened in Chiapas by saying, "Here we go again, these rebels are part of the old Sandinista-Castroite-Marxist-Leninist legacy. Is this what we want for Mexico?" The rebels proved exactly the contrary: Rather than the last rebellion of that type, this was the first postcommunist rebellion in Latin America. (Fuentes, 1994, p. 56.)

This marvelous argument makes an important point; the EZLN insurgency was novel. Yet the features that make it so novel—notably the links to transnational and local NGOs that claim to represent civil society—move the topic largely out of an "insurgency" and into a "netwar" framework. Without the influx of NGO-based social activists, starting hours after the insurrection began, the situation in Chiapas would probably have deteriorated into a conventional insurgency and counterinsurgency, in which the small, poorly equipped EZLN might not have done well, and its efforts at "armed propaganda" would not have seemed out of the ordinary.

Transnational NGO activism attuned to the information age, not the nature of the EZLN insurgency per se, is what changed the framework. The EZLN was not a "wired" indigenous army. In Marcos, it had a superb media spokesman, but the guerrillas did not have their own laptop computers, Internet connections, fax machines, and cellular telephones. These information-age capabilities were in the hands of most transnational and some Mexican NGOs—and they used them to great effect for conveying the EZLN's and their own views, for communicating and coordinating with each other, and for creating an extraordinary mobilization of support, as laid out in this and the next several chapters.

THREE LAYERS TO THE ZAPATISTA MOVEMENT

In retrospect, Mexico and Chiapas were ripe for social netwar in the early 1990s. Mexico as a whole—its state, economy, and society—was (and still is) in a deep, difficult transition. Traditional clannish and hierarchical patterns of behavior continued to rule the political system. But that system was beginning to open up. Presidents Miguel de la Madrid (1982–1988) and Carlos Salinas de Gortari (1988–1994) had started to liberalize the economy and, to a much lesser degree, the polity. Mexico was beginning to adapt to modern market principles. And independent civil-society actors, including a range of NGOs, were beginning to gain strength and to challenge the government for lagging at democratization and for neglecting social welfare issues.[1]

Meanwhile, Chiapas, once an isolated backwater on Mexico's southern border, was becoming awash with outside forces. It was still characterized by tremendous, age-old gaps between the wealthy and impoverished—kept wide by privileged landowners who ran feudal fiefdoms with private armies, by dictatorial *caciques* (local bosses), and by the plight of poor *indigenas* (indigenous peoples) who wanted their lives improved and their cultures respected. Mexico's neo-liberal economic reforms, especially those instituted by the Salinas administration, made matters much worse for many *indigenas*, and that set the stage for the organization and rise of the EZLN.[2]

---

[1]On civil society and the NGOs, see Fox (1994) and Fox and Hernandez (1992).

[2]Sources consulted include Collier (1994a, 1994b), Gossen (1994), Harvey (1994), Hernandez (1994a, 1994b), Nash (1995), and Ross (1995). Chiapas has a long history of rebelliousness over land issues and was viewed in Mexico City as being filled with truculent *indios*, according to a century-old but still interesting report by Stephens [1841] (1988).

Local economic and social conditions are important, but more to the point for this study is that Chiapas was increasingly subject to a plethora of transnational influences. During the 1980s, it became a crossroads for NGO activists, Roman Catholic liberation-theology priests, Protestant evangelists, Guatemalan refugees, guerrillas from Central America, and criminals trafficking in narcotics and weapons. These transnational forces were stronger and more distinctive in Chiapas than in two other nearby states—Oaxaca and Guerrero— that have been likely locales for guerrilla insurgencies. Transnational NGOs, notably those concerned with human-rights issues, were showing far more interest in conditions in Chiapas, and they had better connections there (mainly through the diocese and related Mexican NGOs in San Cristóbal de las Casas) than they did in Guerrero or Oaxaca.[3] This helps explain why Chiapas and not another state gave rise to an insurgency that became a netwar in 1994.

How, then, did network designs come to define the Zapatista movement? They evolved out of the movement's three layers, each of which is discussed below:

- At the social base of the EZLN are the *indigenas*—indigenous peoples—from several Mayan language and ethnic groups. This layer, the most "tribal," engages ideals and objectives that are very egalitarian, communitarian, and consultative.

- The next layer is found in the EZLN's leadership—those top leaders, mostly from educated middle-class *Ladino* backgrounds, who have little or no Indian ancestry and who infiltrated into Chiapas in order to create a guerrilla army. This was the most hierarchical layer—at least initially—in that the leadership aspired to organize hierarchical command structures for waging guerrilla warfare in and beyond Chiapas.

- The top layer—top from a netwar perspective—consists of the myriad local (Mexican) and transnational (mostly American and

---

[3]In Guerrero and Oaxaca, the *indigena* cultures and structures were also not quite as strong, distinctive, and alienated from the Mexican government as they were in Chiapas.

Canadian) NGOs who rallied to the Zapatista cause. This is the most networked layer from an information-age perspective.[4]

These are very diverse layers, involving actors from disparate cultures who have different values, goals, and strategic priorities. This is far from a monolithic or uniform set of actors. No single, formalized organizational design or doctrine characterizes it—or could be imposed on it for long. The shape and dynamics of the Zapatista movement unfolded in quite an ad hoc manner.

The social netwar qualities of the Zapatista movement depend mainly on the top layer, that of the NGOs. Without it, the EZLN would probably have settled into a mode of organization and behavior more like a classic insurgency or ethnic conflict. Indeed, the capacity of the EZLN and of the overall Zapatista movement to mount information operations, an essential feature of social netwar, depended heavily on the attraction of the NGOs to the EZLN's cause, and on the NGOs' ability to impress the media and use faxes, e-mail, and other telecommunications systems for spreading the word. But the nature of the base layer, the *indigenas*, also drove the EZLN in network directions, as discussed below. These distinctions about the layers are significant for sorting out which aspects of the Zapatista movement correspond to netwar, and which do not.

THE *INDIGENAS*: GROWING DESPERATION AND POLITICIZATION

Chiapas is among Mexico's poorest, most marginalized states.[5] By most measures of misery, it scores far worse than the Mexican average.[6] The EZLN's local agenda—for better education and medical

---

[4]Not much is done in this study with the point that tribal, hierarchical, and networked forms of organization have coexisted within the Zapatista movement. But for an explanation as to why this point may be significant, and a hint that more might be done with the point, see Ronfeldt (1996).

[5]Sources consulted include Arizpe (1996), Collier (1994a, 1994b), Gonzalez Casanova (1996), Orozco (1995), Pazos (1994), Tello (1995), Trejo (1994), and Villafuerte and Garcia (1994).

[6]For example, the portion of people in Chiapas who live in homes with dirt floors is 51 percent; the national figure is 21 percent. The figure for people earning more than the minimum wage is 41 percent in Chiapas, and 73 percent for Mexico at large. Even

services, electricity, paved roads, etc.—resonated with the *indigenas* because of the awful poverty and desperation in the region.

The EZLN's social base consists mostly of *indigenas* from Mayan language groups and communities known as Tzotzil, Tzeltal, Tojolabal, and Chole. There are other Mayan groups, but these were the ones whose migration into the eastern lowlands and whose historical presence in the central highlands meant they ended up squarely in the EZLN's recruiting zone.

The paragraphs that follow appear to emphasize the effects of adverse economic factors and policies on the *indigenas*. But it is important to realize that the key economic factor—land—is not really about economics from an indigenous viewpoint. As one of our interviewees (Donna Lee Van Cott) explained, land matters intensely to Indians because it is the physical basis for community—for having a sense of community and for being able to endure as a community. Without land, an indigenous people cannot dwell together; their community is culturally dead. Outsiders (including Marxists) often view the Indian struggle for land in economic class terms, evoking images of "landless peasants." But for Indians, the truly important dimensions of the land issue are about community and culture. Thus, in Chiapas, the *indigenas* who migrated ever deeper into the jungle were striving not only to earn a living, but also to find a way to preserve community.[7]

Against this background, a multifaceted economic crisis in the 1980s prompted many *indigenas* to embrace the EZLN. This crisis attacked the indigenous population in all areas vital to their survival. First, continuing migration from other regions inside and outside Chiapas aggravated existing land pressures. Except for the fertile valleys in the western and southwestern parts, much of Chiapas is unsuited for farming; it is either mountainous highlands or heavily forested jungle that does not remain fertile after deforestation. Migration into the

---

these figures mask the high percentage of the population lacking basic services in the poorest areas. In nearly 15 percent of Chiapas's 111 municipalities, over 70 percent of the population lack electricity, drainage, or toilets. One index of marginalization shows that 85 percent of the state lives in a desperate condition. In a five-tiered ranking system of low to very high marginalization, 38 municipalities rank very high and 56 high.

[7]Also see Van Cott (1996), p. 70.

eastern portion of the state began in the 1950s as *indigenas* from the highlands moved hopefully (even inspired by Catholic priests to believe they were taking part in a modern Exodus) into the Lacandón jungle in search of land. But their situation was soon aggravated by large flows of people from other states. Then, in 1968, a decree from Mexico City appeased peasant protesters elsewhere in Mexico by granting them land in Chiapas. In 1972, another decree granted a huge tract of land to a local non-Mayan tribe, the Lacandones, precisely where the Mayan migrants had settled. In 1978, yet another decree authorized the creation of a biosphere reserve in the area. All this exacerbated land pressures, and land disputes, for the Mayan populace.[8]

The *indigenas* suffered still another major setback when the Salinas administration amended Article 27 of Mexico's constitution in a way that stripped peasants of their hope for the future. For decades, Article 27 had provided for land reform and redistribution, and as anthropologist George Collier (1994b, p. 30) notes, redistributive policies were a major factor in maintaining peace in a region where so many other factors favored rebellion:

> It is difficult to overstate the power of land reform in winning peasants to the side of the State. Even when land reforms were agonizingly slow in coming—and they often were—the federal government was able to hold out the promise of land reform as a way of retaining peasant loyalty.

As part of broader policies to liberalize the national economy, the amendment ended policies and programs that had ensured communal grants to peasant groups in Chiapas. The termination of land reform by this amendment further increased the attractiveness of the EZLN insurgency.

Finally, Mexico's economic liberalization policies of the 1980s and early 1990s created an agricultural crisis for the peasants, for it brought the termination of subsidies and credits and eliminated agencies regulating agricultural policies. Price supports ended, and

---

[8]Although the state's population is only 4 percent of the national total, 25 percent of all land disputes in Mexico are in Chiapas; and 30 percent of all petitions for land presented to the federal government come from Chiapas (Burguete, 1995, p. 9).

the region's most important products—wood, coffee, and cattle—earned far less income. The rural poor suffered from these changes, losing the few programs that had helped them subsist. During the 1980s, the adult working population receiving less than the minimum wage grew by 83 percent (Villafuerte and García, 1994, p. 90). Meanwhile, a sharp fall in coffee prices in international markets, from $180 per hundred pounds in 1986 to $60 in 1992, further aggravated conditions.

As their economic and thus their cultural and social woes mounted from the 1970s onward, the restless *indigenas* formed new peasant organizations that were independent of the federal and state governments and of the ruling political party, the Institutional Revolutionary Party (PRI). A vibrant set of indigenous organizations emerged, the most important being the Unión de Ejidos-Quiptic Ta Lecubtesel, the Unión de Uniones, and a series of organizations best known by their acronyms: ANCIEZ, ARIC (a splinter of the Unión de Uniones), CIOAC, and OCEZ. Their activities ranged from training and education programs, to forming credit unions, to filing petitions and lodging complaints with the authorities, to seizing disputed lands and defiantly trying to hold onto them. Of these organizations, ARIC and ANCIEZ eventually became important recruiting grounds and strongholds of the EZLN and served as cover for some of its activities. However, not all members were pro-EZLN. For example, ARIC, despite a Maoist orientation, was basically reformist and peaceable and would end up losing many members to the EZLN. Indeed, "even as the EZLN was nourished by the movements mentioned above, the great majority of the activists and organizations in the state decided not to actively participate in the armed uprising" (Burguete, 1995, p. 11).

Meanwhile, from the 1970s onward, radical elements of the Catholic Church stationed in Chiapas gained a powerful presence among the *indigenas*. The Diocese of San Cristóbal de las Casas in the central highlands, headed by Samuel Ruíz (known in some circles as the "Red Bishop"), became a key player in the mobilization and politicization of the *indigenas*, notably with the organization of the landmark Indigenous Encounter in 1974 that stirred many Mayans to engage in the kinds of organizing noted above. Moreover, the preaching of liberation theology by many (but not all) Dominican, Marist, and to a lesser extent, Jesuit priests would eventually encourage rebellion. Ruíz and some other priests favored church teachings about helping poor people regain their dignity and rights (termed the "option for the poor"), and some also preached liberation theology (which went beyond the "option for the poor" to allow the "just use" of force by the oppressed). Ruíz would describe Salinas-style neo-liberalism and the poverty it spawned as being "totally contrary to the will of God." While his diocese denies having ever funded the EZLN, it acknowledges the justice of its cause. Indeed, the EZLN's founders (as well as organizers of the Unión del Pueblo, another armed movement) were able to penetrate the closed, suspicious indigenous communities and organizations by first approaching them with the assistance of sympathetic priests. The commitment of Ruíz and his followers in the San Cristóbal diocese to the "option for the poor," if not to liberation theology, set them apart from other dioceses in the area where this theology was not as strong nor the priests as committed.

Finally, although the *indigenas* had long suffered from repression, a particularly terrible wave hit them during the 1980s, instituted by then-governor General Absalón Castellanos, who was a very wealthy cattle rancher and leader of an extended family that amounted to one of the most powerful political clans in the state. His ascendance to the governorship and his security policies were partly a result of concerns in Mexico City that guerrilla warfare would spread north-ward from Central America, and that Chiapas needed to be made militarily secure.

These decades of desperation, politicization, and organization among the *indigenas* led to an increasing pool of people ready to opt for armed struggle. At the turn of the decade, repression eased a bit, and the Salinas administration poured resources into Chiapas by way of its welfare-oriented National Solidarity Program. Moreover, the revolutionary trend in Central America abated, the Sandinista regime lost power in Nicaragua, and the Soviet Union collapsed—all leading to a spread of assumptions that socialism was dead or dying. None of this was good for the EZLN or for its relations with ARIC or the diocese, the two major forces for radical reform in the area. Many communities were divided, or undecided, as to whether to opt for armed struggle or to stick with pressing for peaceful change (Womack, 1997, p. 46). But by then a hard core had developed in and around the EZLN, and it was still attracting and retaining widespread indigenous support, especially among the youngest of the disaffected and among women.[9] By its own count, the EZLN figured its forces numbered 12, 000 at the beginning of 1993, on the eve of deciding to go to war.

THE EZLN: MIXTURE OF VERTICAL AND HORIZONTAL DESIGNS

The origins of the EZLN remain unclear. From what is known (mostly from Tello (1995) and Womack (1997)),[10] the movement began in the 1980s as a very different kind of organization from what emerged in 1994. Its initial, hierarchical design was remolded by its contacts with the *indigenas* and later the NGOs.

The EZLN is evidently mainly an offspring of the Fuerzas de Liberación Nacional (FLN), a little-known clandestine group founded by young intellectual radicals from Northern Mexico who had been preparing, with little success, for armed struggle in Mexico. Members of two lesser revolutionary groups, the Unión del Pueblo[11] and the Linea Proletaria faction of Política Popular,[12] played secondary roles in the creation of the EZLN. Like many other armed groups of the time, the FLN formed in reaction to the government's massacre of students in Tlatelolco in 1968. Initially, it had ties with other armed groups, but these were severed as the FLN eschewed their

---

[9]The material on indigenous organizing and on liberation theology is largely from Tello (1995), but also see Burguete (1995), Gonzalez Casanova (1996), Guillermoprieto (1995), Van Cott (1996), Womack (1997), and other sources. On the role of women and women's issues, see Stephen (1996).

[10]Some activists we interviewed criticized Tello (1995) for reputedly relying partly on Mexican intelligence materials and for not using with complete accuracy some of the field interviews he conducted. Yet this work remains the single most impressive, professional, and informative source to date. Also see Womack (1997).

[11]The role of the Unión del Pueblo (People's Union) reappears later in the story with the emergence of the Popular Revolutionary Army (EPR). The EPR is partly an offspring of the Clandestine Workers Revolutionary Party "People's Union" (PROCUP), which still exists and which is itself an outgrowth of the original Unión del Pueblo. See the discussion later in this report.

[12]Leaders of Linea Proletaria, who favored peaceful over armed change, would be coopted by the Salinas administration, and they would gain considerable influence in ARIC as well as in the government's National Solidarity Program, which dispensed resources in the region.

hasty recruitment practices, assaults, and kidnappings. The FLN favored a low profile and a long gestation, with careful recruiting and a slow development of support among the peasantry—a Maoist approach.

In the mid-1970s, the FLN began training in the Chiapas jungles (initially without contact with the *indigenas* or radical priests there). However, the police and army dealt a severe blow to the FLN in 1974, necessitating a slow rebuilding over the next decade. When the FLN reemerged, at its head were guerrillas who would become key players in the EZLN, notably Germán, Marcos, and Elisa. The reconstituted FLN, which had cells in various parts of Mexico, defined its goal as socialism, to be achieved by combining proletarian battles with those of the peasants and the *indigenas*. Its 1983 statutes called for creating the EZLN by name; that year, key FLN leaders moved into the Chiapas jungle to accomplish this, at a time when liberation theology was vibrant, some tiny cadres associated with other guerrilla groups already existed, hopes were rising that revolution would triumph in Central America and spread into Mexico via Chiapas, and peasant organizations like ARIC existed that might be infiltrated. The FLN leadership aimed to establish a powerful center of operations in Chiapas, while also creating a nationwide infrastructure of armed cells.

The founders had a hierarchical design in mind for creating the EZLN as a key *foco* and linking (if not subordinating) it to a national directorate under the command of the FLN. But their ideological and organizational frameworks had little meaning or relevance to the *indigenas* they encountered and aimed to recruit. Consequently, as the EZLN interacted with the *indigenas* and their organizations, as well as with the local priests—indeed, people associated with the EZLN, ARIC, and the diocese all became quite well known to each other—the EZLN began to adopt some of the characteristics of indigenous social organizations.

The *indigenas* disapproved of hierarchical command structures. They wanted flat, decentralized designs that emphasized consultation at the community level. Indeed, their key social concepts are about community and harmony—the community is supposed to be the center of all social activity, and its institutions are supposed to maintain harmony among family members, residents of the village, and the spiritual and material worlds. Decisionmaking is essentially communal, and the key positions of power in a village belong to a larger council, under the notion that many people make better decisions than just one (see Maurer, 1995).

> [I]n general, the indigenas did not consider themselves to be sovereign individuals in a society but organic members of a community. They argued for hours and hours, entire nights, for months and months, before arriving at what they called *the agreement*. On reaching the agreement, those who were against it had no option; either they followed along with the rest, or they left the community.[13]

In this design, the purpose of power and authority is to serve the community, not to command it—so one who does not know how to serve cannot know how to govern. Marcos would learn this and later point out that he could not give an order—his order would simply not exist—if it had not been authorized by an assembly or a committee representing the *indigenas*. While elements of hierarchy are found in these indigenous structures, the Mexican federal and state structures in the region are terribly hierarchical by comparison and are thus viewed as alien impositions.

During the 1980s, a whole variety of factors—the economic crisis noted above; the wave of repression inflicted by the governor, the landlords, and their paramilitary forces; the liberationist preachings of Catholic priests; and the difficulties of gaining relief through existing peasant organizations—all led to recruiting and organizing opportunities for the EZLN's founders. At first, this was done in the name of self-defense, a goal that resonated well with the *indigenas* and priests; only later did the goal become liberation and revolution. As recruitment and organization advanced—and to assure they kept advancing—the EZLN's founders adapted their principles to those of the *indigenas*.[14] The EZLN did not copy their organizational forms, but it did begin to resemble them. This must not have been an easy

---

[13]Tello (1995), p. 184, translation. Some communities were indeed divided over whether to support the looming insurgency, and some families were expelled and their belongings redistributed after the pro-EZLN vote won.

[14]Sources include Maurer (1995), Ross (1995), Tello (1995), Van Cott (1996), Womack (1997), and an interview with Jose Arellano, Mexico City, March 5, 1996.

transition for all the EZLN's leaders to make. As late as its first major manifesto calling people to arms, "El Despertador Mexicano" (The Mexican Awakening), issued December 1, 1993, the EZLN describes itself as having a hierarchical, centralized command structure (Van Cott, 1996, p. 75). However, Marcos soon clarified that

> Armed struggle has to take place where the people are, and we faced the choice of continuing with a traditional guerrilla structure, or *masificando* and putting the strategic leadership in the hands of the people. Our army became scandalously Indian, and there was a certain amount of clashing while we made the adjustment from our orthodox way of seeing the world in terms of "bourgeois and prole-tarians" to the community's collective democratic conceptions, and their world view. (Quoted by Guillermoprieto, 1995, p. 39.)

This shows up in the appearance of the Clandestine Revolutionary Indigenous Committees (CCRIs) in the midst of the EZLN command structure—see Figure 2—and in the CCRIs' dependence on consul-tations with community assemblies outside that structure. In Jan-uary 1993, the FLN/EZLN leadership gathered to vote on when to go to war. One position held that the time was still not ripe—the FLN had too few forces in northern and central Mexico, the army was capable of focusing just on Chiapas, and thus it was advisable to keep organizing and preparing for even another ten years. The position that Marcos favored was to go on the offensive as soon as possible, before local reformist organizations receiving government monies could attract the EZLN's following away, before the army went on the attack based on its growing intelligence about the EZLN, and so that the EZLN could take advantage of 1994 being a year for national elections. This latter position won out. Marcos then proposed that a CCRI be created for the purpose of consulting with community assemblies about supporting the EZLN's decision to go to war. Soon, the (often split) votes taken in assemblies in March 1993 rendered the authority that the EZLN was looking for.[15] The CCRIs, which grew in number, were not part of the EZLN's original design. It was supposed to be headed by the General Command; but, according to

---

[15]From Tello (1995) and Womack (1997), who talk about a vote in January 1993. Other sources, including Marcos, refer to a vote in 1992.

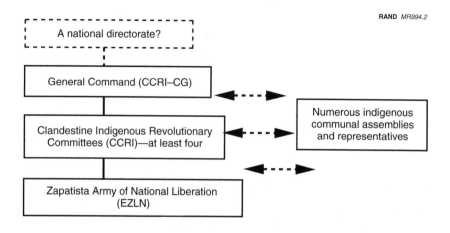

Figure 2—EZLN Organization

Marcos and others, its authority was soon subordinated to the approval of the CCRIs.

Thus, one Zapatista noted, the movement was not born democratic, but "the form and organization of the indigenous communities permeated and dominated our movement and we had to democratize the Indian way." It might be added that the EZLN and the broader Zapatista movement also ended up having to democratize the NGO way.

ACTIVIST NGOs: GLOBAL, REGIONAL, AND LOCAL NETWORKS

To understand why a social netwar emerged in Mexico—and why an insurgency mutated into a social netwar—the analyst must look at trends outside Mexico involving activist NGOs.[16] Such NGOs, most of which play both service and advocacy roles, are not a new phe-

---

[16]Here, the term NGO includes many nonprofit organizations (NPOs), private voluntary organizations (PVOs), and grass-roots organizations (GROs). It does not include international governmental organizations (IGOs), and what are sometimes referred to as government-organized NGOs (GONGOs), government-inspired NGOs (GINGOs), and quasi-NGOs (QUANGOs).

nomenon. But their numbers, diversity, and strength have increased dramatically around the world since the 1970s. And mainly since the 1980s, they have developed information-age organizational and technological networks for connecting and coordinating with each other.[17] Thus, the NGOs' ability to swarm into Mexico in response to the EZLN's insurrection was no anomaly; it stemmed from a confluence of network-building efforts spread over a decade or two at global, regional, and local levels. [18]

Some of the activist NGOs were more radical and militant than others, and some were more affected by old ideologies than others. But, altogether, most were in basic agreement that they were not interested in seeking political power or in helping other actors seek power. Rather, they wanted to foster a form of democracy in which civil-society actors would be strong enough to counterbalance state and market actors and could play central roles in making public-policy decisions that affect civil society (see Frederick, 1993a). This relatively new ideological stance, a by-product of the information revolution, was barely emerging on the eve of the EZLN insurrection, but we surmise that it had enough momentum among activists to help give coherence to the swarm that would rush into Mexico, seeking to help pacify as well as protect the EZLN.

Two story lines about issue-oriented NGOs are significant here. One is about the growth of issue-networks[19] that focus on *specific* issues, like human rights. The other is about the rise of issue-networks that engage *multiple* issues, as in efforts to oppose U.S. policy in Central America in the 1980s. The two story lines converge, but we discuss them separately here for presentational ease. Undergirding and paralleling both story lines about issue-oriented NGOs is another story about the growth of infrastructure-building NGOs; what matters to them is building the organizational and technological links for networking among activist NGOs, almost regardless of what specific issue concerns each one. The remainder of this chapter

---

[17]Ronfeldt (1996) cites documentation for this general phenomenon. Mathews (1997) and Slaughter (1997) are significant additions to the literature.

[18]Our background comes in part from Frederick (1993b) and other chapters in Ronfeldt, Thorup, Aguayo, and Frederick (1993).

[19]Term from Sikkink (1993), as discussed above.

considers the status of all these types of NGOs on the eve of the EZLN insurrection.[20] The next chapter discusses their ensuing actions.

The growth of two specific issue-networks—the human-rights and indigenous-rights networks—is particularly important for explaining the Zapatista netwar. As Kathryn Sikkink (1993) shows, the human-rights network was growing at global and regional levels by the mid-1980s, when it began to focus on conditions in Mexico. At the time, Mexico's own human-rights network was in a fledgling state; but partly because of its becoming connected to the transnational network, it quickly expanded. About four human-rights NGOs existed in Mexico in 1984, sixty in 1991, and "by 1993 there were over two hundred independent human-rights monitoring and advocacy NGOs."[21]

Meanwhile, the indigenous-rights network was also expanding up and down the Americas (particularly in Canada). While "the indigenous nations of the Americas have a strong tradition of building communication and media networks to support their self-determination goals" since the 19th century (O'Donnell and Delgado, 1995), a surge in transnational networking gained momentum following the First Continental Encounter of Indigenous Peoples in 1990 in Ecuador, and after the formation of the Continental Coordinating Commission of Indigenous Nations and Organizations (CONIC) at a meeting in 1991 in Panama. Although pan-Mayan aspirations figure little in the EZLN's goals, a pan-Mayan movement was emerging in parts of Central America and Southern Mexico without regard for national boundaries. It reflected the diffuse nonhierarchical structures of the network and was "linked by radio broadcasting, publications, telephone calls and faxes and, increasingly by Internet e-mail" (O'Donnell and Delgado, 1995).[22]

Overall, these indigenous-rights networks seek to promote self-determination and autonomy as their goals, but they often adjust

---

[20]Cleaver (1994a, 1995c) provides an illuminating discussion of how the Zapatista networking drew its strength from the earlier types of networking discussed in this chapter, and his writings are part of the basis for our discussion.

[21]An accounting by Mexico's National Human Rights Commission (CNDH) holds that the number of human-rights NGOs in Mexico grew from 191 in November 1993 to 376 in May 1996.

[22]Also see Van Cott (1996).

their issue orientation to fit the priorities of their audiences. At times, this has meant emphasizing human rights, at other times environmental issues. Thus, Alison Brysk (1994, p. 36) finds that

> The Indian rights movement consciously repositioned itself in response to these differences in regime responsiveness. As a representative of the flagship advocacy group Cultural Survival noted, "We see ourselves as a human rights organization in the broadest sense, and that was certainly our first track of contact with indigenous rights. But we've moved more into ecology . . . clearly it works better."[23]

This flexibility, which appears in many issue-oriented networks, would make it easy for transnational indigenous-rights NGOs to swarm into Chiapas in sympathy with other single-issue NGOs and to mesh with the local indigenous networks and organizations (also see Cleaver, 1994b, 1995c).

Meanwhile, thousands of NGOs were also involved in another current of activity focused on specific issues at the global level: a series of UN-sponsored conferences and parallel NGO forums on global issues. This too strengthened the activists' networks in the 1990s, albeit indirectly with regard to Chiapas. In particular, the UN-sponsored Conference on the Environment and Development—the "Earth Summit"—in Rio de Janeiro in 1992 put NGOs on the map as global activists. Though the conference mainly assembled government officials and representatives of international governmental organizations (IGOs), one to two thousand NGO representatives were invited, and more showed up. The key event for them was less the official conference than the NGO Global Forum that was organized parallel to the conference to enable NGOs to debate issues and adopt policy positions independently of governments (Preston, 1992; Spiro, 1995).[24] Against this background, the U.S. Undersecretary of

---

[23]Also see Brysk (1996).

[24]The political implications of information technology were a key theme. Results included affirming a Communications, Information, and Networking Treaty to declare communication a basic human right (Preston, 1992). An UNCED Information Strategy Project was also approved to build an international electronic information exchange system for NGOs and other users. It is unclear what happened to these proposals.

State for Global Affairs, Timothy Wirth, observed that governments were awakening to the growing influence of the NGOs:

> [T]he heroes, the heroines of Rio were not government leaders, they weren't bureaucrats leading delegations, but they were this vast array of NGOs who would effectively define the issues and were working very hard to get governments to recognize those issues and recognize what the solutions ought to be.[25]

This experience was repeated next at the UN-sponsored Conference on Human Rights in Vienna in 1993, and then the Conference on Population and Development in Cairo in 1994. Cairo's NGO Forum proved larger than Rio's, and at times gained more media coverage than the official conference did. The progression continued with the Conference on Social Development in Copenhagen in 1995, followed by the Conference on Women and Development in Beijing in 1995.

During these conferences, one infrastructure-building NGO proved particularly crucial: the Association for Progressive Communications (APC). It, along with its affiliates (e.g., Peacenet in the United States, Alternex in Brazil) operates the set of Internet-linked computer net- works most used by activists, and thus it played growing roles in facilitating communications by e-mail and fax among the NGOs, and in enabling them to send reports and press releases to officials, jour- nalists, other interested parties, and publics around the world (Preston, 1992; Whaley, 1995).

The second, overlapping story line is about the growth of *multiple* issue-networks that focus on a generally urgent policy matter. Around Mexico, the development of two multiple issue-networks— one dealing with Central America, the other with NAFTA—is most relevant to accounting for the advent of a social netwar in Mexico.

The first developed in the 1970s–1980s, when numerous, small, mainly leftist and center-leftist NGOs got involved in the conflicts in Central America. Their activities varied from providing humanitar- ian relief and monitoring human-rights abuses, to providing alterna-

---

[25]From "Global Affairs Workshop with Timothy Wirth, Undersecretary of State for Global Affairs," State Department, Washington D.C., June 23, 1994, as reported by Reuters Transcripts, CQ's Washington Alert.

tive sources of news to the media and opposing U.S. policy. The key umbrella networking organization was the innovative, multilayered Committee in Solidarity with the People of El Salvador (CISPES), which spanned a range of peace, human-rights, and church organizations.[26] Activists who had access to the insurgents in El Salvador could sometimes get news of a human-rights abuse into the media faster than U.S. officials could learn of it from their own sources. Indeed, fax machines and e-mail systems enabled the NGOs to move news out of El Salvador and into the media, to inundate U.S. government inboxes with protests and petitions, and to counter what the activists regarded as disinformation and deception campaigns by officials in the Central American region. CISPES was a relatively weak but nonetheless seminal effort to build a transnational network for social netwar.[27]

After the Central American conflicts receded as a front-burner issue and CISPES was becoming less active, the proposal for NAFTA arose. This reanimated the activists' networks and catalyzed a new round of network building. Besides holding face-to-face conferences, NGOs across North America—mainly Canadian and American, but also with nascent Mexican participation[28]—convened conferences and communicated with increasing ease via faxes and computer systems (notably Peacenet) to strategize about their opposition to NAFTA. The participants included activists who had supported CISPES, but participation broadened to include moderates concerned with North American labor and environmental issues. The NGOs' positions varied from opposing the agreement entirely, to proposing the inclusion of a European-style social charter, to seeking influence over specific issues and insisting that issues like labor and the environment be included for the negotiating process to be acceptable. In the end, this diverse array of views and participants coalesced around one key objective: to oppose fast-track approval of NAFTA by the

---

[26]Background appears in Diane Green, "The CISPES Solidarity Model," as posted electronically to Peacenet conferences on May 19–20, 1994, and then circulated on the Internet.

[27]Perhaps in emulation, a Committee in Solidarity with the People of Mexico was recently formed, but it appears to be quite weak.

[28]A leading example of Mexican participation is the Mexican Network Against Free Trade (Red Mexicana de Acción Frente al Libre Comercio—RMALC), which is a co-ordinating center for a number of individual NGOs.

U.S. Congress, but not to explicitly oppose the agreement itself (Thorup, 1991, 1995).

It is difficult to say how influential the NGOs were; they affected some public debates and congressional views, especially on environmental issues, but did not prevent fast-track approval of NAFTA in late 1993. Still, the activists' trinational pan-issue networks got better organized than ever before. This laid a foundation for the rapid NGO mobilization that followed the EZLN insurrection in January 1994, just months after the NAFTA-related activities subsided. The infrastructure was sitting there, with more potential than ever, waiting to be reactivated.

Meanwhile, in Mexico the number, variety, and influence of local NGOs and related organizations had been growing rapidly since the mid-1980s, including in Chiapas, where the Catholic Church played a vital role in the creation and survival of many local NGOs.[29] The rise of Mexican human-rights and indigenous-rights NGOs was briefly discussed above. In addition, pro-democracy NGOs and networks also began to take shape in this period. In their case too, the dynamics of transnational networking is evident. According to Denise Dresser,

> the Mexican pro-democracy movement has developed a two-pronged strategy that combines political theater in Mexico (which mobilizes domestic and international awareness), with lobbying in the United States and collaboration with international organizations. . . . International actors and forces are an integral part of this network, whose power and influence continues to evolve. External pressure has proven to be most effective when it intersects with domestic actors pushing for political change. (Dresser, 1994, pp. 26, 35.)

As parts of the Mexican political system slowly opened up, it became vulnerable to civil-society activism. Even though the state remained undemocratic in many areas, it was increasingly the case that "social

---

[29]We do not say much about the rise of Mexican NGOs, partly to keep a focus on the transnational NGOs. For background on Mexican NGOs, see Fox and Hernandez (1992) and Barry (1992). On pro-democracy networking, see Dresser (1994). As noted, Sikkink (1993) covers human-rights NGOs. Writings in preparation by Sergio Aguayo will add to this literature.

movements can gnaw at small cracks in the system and try and open them further" (Fox, 1994, p. 183). Once a crack is opened up, NGOs can move in to exploit it.

Thus, by the time of the EZLN's insurrection, the transnational NGOs that had been building global and regional networks, notably those concerned with human rights, indigenous rights, and ecumenical and pro-democracy issues, had counterparts to link with in Mexico City, San Cristóbal de las Casas, and other locales. Then, as NGO representatives swarmed into Chiapas in early 1994, new Mexican NGOs were created to assist with communication and coordination among the NGOs—most importantly, the Coalition of Non-Governmental Organizations for Peace (CONPAZ), based at the diocese in San Cristóbal.[30] (An NGO named the National Commission for Democracy in Mexico was established in the United States, but it was basically a public-relations arm for the EZLN.)

Were the EZLN's leaders aware of this potential? Did they foresee that numerous NGOs would swarm to support them? We have no evidence of this. Yet conditions in Chiapas were well known to activists. Amnesty International and Americas Watch had each published a similar report of human-rights violations in the area, the former in 1986, the latter in 1991. Minnesota Advocates for Human Rights and the World Policy Institute published a joint report in August 1993 about soldiers beating and torturing a group of *indigenas* in May 1993. And the Jesuit Refugee Service, long active in the area to deal with Guatemalan refugee issues, became alarmed about the treatment of the *indigenas* in Chiapas and issued an "Urgent Call to the International Community" in August 1993. The Jesuits' demands are nearly identical to those voiced a few months later by many Mexican and transnational NGOs in January 1994.

---

[30]CONPAZ was formed by fourteen Mexican human-rights groups that were active in Chiapas before January. They came together because they were troubled by the outbreak of war, wanted to promote peace, knew they would be more influential if they united, and lacked funding to operate well independently. CONPAZ's aims included coordinating the delivery of emergency supplies and services in the conflict zone, monitoring and denouncing human-rights violations, keeping communication with affected communities, and generating international visibility for NGO activities.

ON THE EVE OF WAR

What we see, then, is the emergence of a movement comprising several layers. The *indigenas* and the NGOs preferred nonhierarchical, network forms of organization and action, while the EZLN was drawn in this direction despite tendencies, as in any traditional Marxist armed movement, to want a hierarchy at its core. This overall bias in favor of nonhierarchical designs made for affinities—and uneasy alliances—that would facilitate the mobilization of the NGOs on behalf of the EZLN and the *indigenas* and contribute to the solidarity of the movement once mobilized. Moreover, by the end of 1993, strong organizational and technological networks were in place to sustain a multilayered mobilization.

The insurrection on New Year's Day, 1994, was so surprising that most observers presumed there had been an intelligence failure on the part of the government and the army, even though the army had inklings of the EZLN's existence during 1993. Was it a failure of detection? Of analysis? Or of not getting the analysis into the right hands in Mexico City? How could the army not know? In 1997, two generals revealed in press interviews[31] that the army and the Salinas government, at least at the cabinet level, had known of the EZLN's existence for eight months in 1993. As is often the pattern in Mexican history (see Radu, 1997), the government maneuvered to talk with the EZLN's leadership, using archbishop Ruíz as an interlocutor, in order to prevent an armed rebellion and seek a peaceful outcome. The army was instructed to avoid combat and to collect and provide information to top officials about conditions in Chiapas. Meanwhile, cabinet officials began visiting Chiapas, and a large-scale social and economic assistance program was begun—the very one that Marcos had worried would attract adherents away from the EZLN if it did not start its war soon.

---

[31]The key source is the newspaper article by Francisco Arroyo, "Duraron ocho meses las platicas, revela Godinez," *El Universal,* July 21, 1997—as circulated on the Internet.

Chapter Four

MOBILIZATION FOR CONFLICT

The insurrection did not begin as a social netwar. It began as a rather traditional, Maoist insurgency. But that changed within a matter of a few days as, first, the EZLN's military strategy for waging a "war of the flea" ran into trouble, and second, an alarmed mass of Mexican and transnational NGO activists mobilized and descended on Chiapas and Mexico City in "swarm networks" (term from Kelly, 1994). Meanwhile, no matter how small a territory the EZLN held in Chiapas, it quickly occupied more space in the media than had any other insurgent group in Mexico's if not the world's history.[1]

THE EZLN IN COMBAT—A "WAR OF THE FLEA"

The EZLN's leaders may be credited with intelligence, flexibility, and innovation for working with indigenous ideas and institutions. Marcos in particular succeeded at adapting the EZLN's world views to those of the Maya. Even so, the EZLN—as a small guerrilla force confronting a far stronger state opponent—evidently intended, at least initially, to pursue a very traditional strategy of armed struggle: a "war of the flea" (a term popularized by Taber (1970) and repeated in regard to Chiapas by Ross (1995)).

This is often an optimal design for small, lightly armed, irregular forces. It allows insurgents to keep the initiative through surprise attacks by small units, following Mao's dictum of combining central

---

[1]Point adapted from writings by Mexican commentator Carlos Montemayor (e.g., "La Rebellion Indigena," *La Jornada Semanal*, February 9, 1997).

strategic control with tactical decentralization (see Griffith, 1961, p. 114). Acts of sabotage against Mexico's economic infrastructure were to be features of the FLN/EZLN's campaign plan. Victory in such a war would hinge on the ability of dispersed operational units (like the *focos* of Ernesto "Che" Guevara's theory of guerrilla warfare—see Guevara [1960], 1985) to pursue a common strategic goal, strike at multiple targets in a coordinated manner, and share scarce resources with each other through strategic and logistical alliances.

This strategic approach has antecedents throughout the history of Mexican wars and struggles for independence (Asprey, 1994, pp. 159–171). Emiliano Zapata, to whom the EZLN owes its name, waged a flea-like guerrilla war that played an important role in determining the outcome of the Mexican Revolution. Guerrilla operations were key forms of resistance in earlier periods as well, against both the Spanish drive (1815–1825) to maintain control over this part of its overseas empire in the wake of the Napoleonic Wars and the French effort to rule Mexico in the 1860s. Each time, guerrilla warfare succeeded against powerful opponents. The EZLN's leadership was cognizant of these historic episodes and of earlier uses of guerrilla warfare techniques by the Indians who had resisted the Spanish conquest in the 16th century.[2]

When the EZLN commenced hostilities on January 1, 1994, it thus continued in the long guerrilla-warfare traditions of Mexican insurgency and resistance. And, like so many previous movements, it quickly found itself in trouble—perhaps by adhering too closely to the basic tenets of the "war of the flea."

---

[2]For the *Mexica*, as the Aztecs referred to themselves, guerrilla tactics emerged naturally, as a way to counter the Spanish invaders' advantages in firepower, cavalry, and body armor. As Prescott ([1843] 1949, p. 428) put it, "In the open field, they were no match for the Spaniards." Yet this deficiency drove the Indians to innovate, even to diverge from their own military traditions. Thus, "The *Mexica* themselves were fighting a different kind of war . . . all just fought as best they could, without many orders, but with instinctive discipline" (Thomas, 1993, p. 400). This drove the conquistadors to make doctrinal adjustments of their own, the most prominent being a shift from their traditional close-packed formations to what Bernal Díaz ([1568], 1963, pp. 353, 364) recalled, in his memoir, as a more loosely knit "skirmishing" approach. This was made necessary by the firepower of the guerrilla bands: "The enemy discharged so many stones from their slings, so many darts, and so many arrows, that although all our soldiers wore armor, they were wounded." Despite the hard fighting, the Spanish doctrinal innovation paid off with complete victory.

Two major problems emerged, one at the organizational level, the other at the tactical. First, at the outset of its campaign, the EZLN organized itself into just a few units of almost battalion size (500–700 fighters), which was the optimal battle formation according to Mao (Griffith, 1961, p. 80). While separate detachments were formed out of these larger units, they remained under central command and control, which left them with little initiative to pursue further action in the wake of their occupations of the small towns in Chiapas. Consequently, much of the Zapatista force simply sat in place until orders were given to retreat into the Lacandón jungle. Also, these dispersed detachments were simply too far away to come to the aid of the main forces in a timely manner when the latter came under attack by the Mexican army.

This dispersion of the fighting forces turned out to be a serious problem for the main EZLN components, as it bled off fighters at a time when the EZLN fully expected to be engaging in pitched battles. Indeed, their tactical doctrine was also much influenced by Mao, whose dictum was that "Guerrillas concentrate when the enemy is advancing upon them" (from Griffith, 1961, p. 103). For example, in the firefight in the Ocosingo market the EZLN units stood their ground, with most of one operating field unit, comprising hundreds of fighters, engaging the Mexican army openly. The results were disastrous, as the insurgents were quickly pinned down and exposed to heavy fire from artillery and helicopters. There is some evidence that the EZLN military leadership tried to avoid this engagement by calling for a prompt retreat, but the Zapatista commander on the ground in Ocosingo continued to follow what he took to be his standing orders, and EZLN casualties were very high (scores dead, over one hundred wounded).[3]

EZLN leaders quickly became aware of the flaws in their traditional guerrilla strategy, and they promptly began adapting. They retreated from their exposed positions in the cities and towns and dissolved their large combat units, replacing them with much smaller fighting bands of roughly squad size (12–16 men). Their doctrine of open confrontation, which they expected would spark a national uprising

---

[3]Tello (1995) is a useful source on the first days of the fighting. The authors thank an anonymous Mexican military intelligence official for his comments on the EZLN's organization and doctrine.

(which showed no signs of emerging),[4] was replaced with a series of ambushes and minor skirmishes. Combat operations were thus dying out, and when the public, the media, and human-rights NGOs, both domestic and transnational, got involved, the EZLN was ready to shift gears to a very different sort of conflict in which the principal maneuvers would take place off the battlefield.

At this point, since we argue that a shift from guerrilla warfare to social netwar occurred, we should note the differences between the two. There are many, and they span the spectrum from political purpose to military tactics. Guerrilla operations, for example, are generally waged with the aim of overthrowing the existing order, making it an important subset of the larger phenomenon of revolutionary warfare (see Griffith, 1961; Guevara [1960], 1985; Shy and Collier, 1986). Indeed, a key element in guerrilla campaigns is the winning over of increasingly larger segments of society, eventually providing the wherewithal to confront the existing order openly.

Moreover, guerrilla forces, to succeed, are thought to require integration with, or evolution into, regular forces capable of fighting pitched battles or of launching the sort of blitzkrieg that the North Vietnamese erstwhile guerrillas did in the spring of 1975. Mao held the view that only "guerrilla operations correlated with those of our regular forces will produce victory" (cited in Griffith, 1961, p. 70). If one lacks conventional forces, then one must find outside allies with such capabilities. In his survey of the history of guerrilla warfare, Gann (1971) concludes that the lack of such conventional combat capabilities was the most common cause of failure in the "war of the flea." Taber's analysis of the failures of guerrilla campaigns by the Huks and the Malayan communists makes this same point about the need for conventional fighting forces (Taber, 1970, pp. 120–130).

The ultimate guerrilla aim of overthrowing the opponent in pitched battle has distinctive organizational, strategic, and doctrinal elements. As mentioned earlier, it is seen as important from the start to organize into larger units, generally of battalion size. These will grow into regiments and divisions that can ultimately confront the enemy

---

[4]The FLN proved to lack a strong nationwide structure. Moreover, despite exhortations by Marcos and other EZLN leaders, no other armed indigenous groups rose up elsewhere in Mexico in this period.

openly. Strategically, the guerrilla campaign follows a sequence of events, moving from rural to urban settings, with campaigning begun in far-off areas but culminating near the opponent's principal locus of power. Tactically, pitched battles are to be fought whenever possible, as the opponent advances upon the guerrillas. These characteristics appear consistently in the major primary sources on guerrilla warfare, as well as among historical analyses of this type of conflict (see Lenin [1916], 1958; Griffith, 1961; Guevara [1960], 1985; Taber, 1970; Gann, 1971; and Asprey, 1994).

By way of contrast, netwar is a different form of conflict. Inasmuch as the key combatants are organized along networked lines, military operations can be conducted by even quite small units, almost always well below the battalion size recommended by theorists of guerrilla war. In terms of political aims, netwar may be waged with a state's overthrow and revolution in mind, but it may easily accommodate a reform agenda as well. It is thus a more discriminate and versatile tool of conflict than guerrilla warfare; and it may proceed even in the absence of mass armies, allies, or widespread popular support among indigenous peoples, all of which are normally necessary conditions for the success of guerrilla warfare.

In doctrinal terms, netwar may also avoid requirements to pursue a particular sequence of operations, such as is seen in guerrilla war's pattern of rural-to-urban fighting or hit-and-run raids, with both being eventually replaced with pitched battles. For armed netwarriors, it is possible, and generally desirable, to strike anywhere, at any time—or not to strike at all, even for long periods; to avoid massing, but to attack in swarms; and to find allies in and draw support from other networked actors. In all these ways, armed netwar differs significantly from guerrilla warfare. And in all these ways, the intended "war of the flea" in Chiapas soon mutated into a full-fledged netwar that had both armed and social dimensions.

The most apparent organizational shift in the EZLN was its decentralization and downsizing of maneuver forces.[5] This took place within weeks of the initial attacks on the cities and towns of Chiapas. The other significant development was the EZLN's campaign to

---

[5]Later, we shall see that the Mexican army decentralized in response. Thus, one type of decentralization was countered by another.

attract NGOs and other members of "global civil society" to their cause. As discussed below, these nonstate actors mobilized quickly, and they helped to constrain the Mexican government's military response to the uprising, even during a period when the United States may have been tacitly interested in seeing a forceful crackdown on the rebels. While reaching out to these nonstate political allies, the EZLN altered its own declaratory political goals, calling explicitly for reform instead of the overthrow of the government. As these changes occurred, the EZLN's "war of the flea" gave way to the Zapatista movement's "war of the swarm."

TRANSNATIONAL NGO MOBILIZATION—A "WAR OF THE SWARM"

As word of the insurrection spread, U.S. and Canadian activist NGOs that had earlier participated in the networks opposing NAFTA and U.S. policy in Central America were among the first to mobilize to express support and sympathy for the EZLN's cause and to criticize the Mexican government's response. Also quick to mobilize were NGOs that belonged to the growing, highly networked human-rights and indigenous-rights movements. Soon a broad array of peace, ecumenical, trade, and other issue-oriented NGOs joined the mobilization.

Establishing a Networked Presence

Within days, delegations were flowing into Mexico City and San Cristóbal de las Casas, where links were established with local NGOs and EZLN representatives. Demonstrations, marches, and peace caravans were organized, not only in Mexico but even in front of Mexican consulates in the United States. The NGOs made good use of computerized conferencing, e-mail, fax, and telephone[6] systems, as well as face-to-face meetings, to communicate and coordinate with each other. They focused on improving their ability to work together (as in the creation of CONPAZ) and began to struggle ceaselessly through fax-writing campaigns, public assemblies, press conferences and interviews, and other measures to make Mexican

---

[6]Cellular telephones could be used in San Cristóbal de las Casas.

officials aware of their presence and put them on notice to attend to selected issues. The fax numbers of Mexican and U.S. officials were often posted in Internet newsgroups and mailing lists; if a number became inoperable, a new one was sometimes discovered and posted. In addition, the activists worked to assure that the insurrection became, and remained, an international media event—swollen by the "CNN effect"—so that the EZLN and its views were portrayed favorably. Indeed, all sides waged public-relations battles to legitimize, delegitimize, and otherwise affect perceptions of each other.

Meanwhile, Marcos and other EZLN leaders kept urging NGO representatives to come to Mexico. Likewise, the NGOs already there began calling for other NGOs to join the mobilization. A kind of "bandwagon effect" took hold. A dynamic swarm grew that aimed to put the Mexican government and army on the defensive. NGO coalitions arose that were characterized by "flexible, conjunctural [*coyuntural*], and horizontal relations" held together by shared goals and demands (Castro, 1994, p. 123).[7]

What did the NGOs demand? The list included the achievement of democracy through nonviolent means; respect for human rights; a cease-fire and withdrawal by the army; peace negotiations, with the local bishop in Chiapas as mediator; freedom of information; and respect for the NGOs' roles, including access to monitor conditions in the conflict zone. Except for the commitment to nonviolence, the NGOs' collective agenda closely resembled the EZLN's. To some extent, this was a compromise agenda. At first, there were tensions (notably in meetings at CONPAZ) between those NGOs that wanted to voice solidarity with the EZLN and those that preferred neutrality. Some activists also had other agendas, notably to achieve the erosion if not the downfall of Mexico's ruling party, the PRI, since it was viewed as the linchpin of all that was authoritarian and wrong in Mexico's political system.[8]

---

[7]Also see Reygadas (1994).

[8]It should be noted that there was a partial disjuncture between some demands of the *indigenas*, which were quite specific and immediate (e.g., electricity), and those of many intellectuals and NGO activists, which were general and sweeping (e.g., electoral reform). In a sense, the *indigenas* and the intellectuals spoke in different languages. The latter generally made for better press.

Many NGO activists sensed they were molding a new model of organization and strategy based on networking that was different from Leninist and other traditional approaches to the creation of social movements. As one keen scholar-activist, Harry Cleaver, states,[9]

> [T]he process of alliance building has created a new organizational form—a multiplicity of rhizomatically connected autonomous groups—that is connecting all kinds of struggles throughout North America that have previously been disconnected and separate. (Cleaver, 1994a.)

> The new organizational forms we see in action are not substitutes for old formulas—Leninist or social democratic. They provide something different: inspiring examples of workable solutions to the post-socialist problem of revolutionary organization and struggle. (Cleaver, 1994b.)

For these information-age activists, nonviolent but compelling action is crucial; to this end, they need rapid, far-reaching communications, as well as freedom of information and travel. Much of the netwar has thus been waged through the media—both old media like newspapers, magazines, and television, and new media like faxes, e-mail, and computer conferencing systems. (Old-fashioned face-to-face and telephone communications were important too.)

Since word of the Zapatista insurrection first spread via the new media, activists made heavy use of the Internet and conferencing systems like Peacenet and Mexico's nascent La Neta (which came on-line in 1993) to disseminate information,[10] to mobilize their forces, and to coordinate joint actions. By the end of 1994, a remarkable number of World Wide Web (WWW) pages, e-mail listserves, and gopher archives had been created on the Internet to convey the

---

[9]Harry Cleaver (1994a) was among the first to identify and discuss the advent of new network designs and to show (1994b) how the NGOs' responses to Chiapas grew out of networking by groups opposed to NAFTA and by groups concerned with the rights of indigenous peoples. Cleaver (1995c) expands on this. When journalist Joel Simon (1995) wrote an article proposing that netwar might be an interesting concept for understanding this model of conflict, a brief storm of discussion followed its circulation on the Internet. See the interesting article by Jason Wehling (1995) and other texts at http://www.teleport.com/~jwehling/OtherNetwars.html.

[10]And sometimes misinformation and disinformation, as discussed later.

EZLN's and Marcos' statements for anyone to read and download,[11] to communicate the views and policy positions of various NGOs, and to show how to conduct what would later be termed "electronic civil disobedience."[12] The Zapatista movement gained an unprecedented transnational presence on the Net, and that presence endures and grows to this day.[13]

While we discuss some limitations of Internet-related activism in the next chapter, it cannot be denied that on-line activities played very important, innovative roles in the "rapid dissemination of information and organization" (phrase from Cleaver, 1997). The organizational effects may be as important as the informational ones. Indeed, many foreign activists evidently believed that without this on-line presence, "the EZLN would not have been able to resist the onslaught of the Mexican state so successfully over the last four years" (Carr, 1997).[14]

Issue-Oriented and Infrastructure-Building NGOs—Both Important

As the netwar got under way, two types of NGOs mobilized in regard to Chiapas, and both were important: (a) issue-oriented NGOs, and (b) infrastructure-building and network-facilitating NGOs. The former receive most of the attention, but the latter are equally important. In a sense, the former correspond to the "content" and the latter to the "conduit"—or the "message" and "medium" respectively—of social activism.

The former type consist of NGOs whose identities and missions revolve around a specific issue area, such as human rights, indigenous

---

[11]An early and famous site, regarded as the EZLN's unofficial home in cyberspace, was established by an American student, Justin Paulson, at http://www.peak.org/ ~justin/ezln/, now located at http://www.ezln.org/.

[12]See Stefan Wray's Web site at http://www.nyu.edu/projects/wray/ecd.html for background and materials on electronic civil disobedience.

[13]The best general guide is Harry Cleaver's Web site, "Zapatistas in Cyberspace: A Guide to Analysis and Resources," at http://www.eco.utexas.edu/faculty/Cleaver/ zapsincyber.html.

[14]Also see Urry (1997), which includes a comparison of the EZLN's media strategies to those of the FMLN in El Salvador in the 1980s.

rights, peace, the environment, or trade and development. Numerous NGOs were active in each such issue area.

For example, in 1994 Chiapas engaged the attention of myriad NGOs concerned with the rights of indigenous peoples: transnational NGOs with no national identity, like the Continental Coordinating Commission of Indigenous Nations (CONIC), the Independent Front of Indian Peoples (FIPI), and the International Indigenous Treaty Council (IITC); U.S.-based NGOs, like the South and Mesoamerican Indian Information Center (SAIIC); Canadian NGOs, like Okanaga Nation; and Mexican NGOs (or quasi-NGOs), such as the State Coalition of Indigenous and Campesino Organizations (CEOIC), the Coordinadora de Organizaciones en Lucha del Pueblo Maya para Su Liberación (COLPUMALI), and the Organización Indigena de los Altos de Chiapas (ORIACH). Many of these have links to each other; for example, COLPULMALI and ORIACH are sister organizations in FIPI-Mexico, and FIPI is a member of CONIC.

The indigenous-rights NGOs responded quickly after the conflict broke out. According to an indigenous-issues journal, "only ten days after the first shots were fired, every major Indian organization met in San Cristóbal de las Casas to form—along with nonindigenous *campesino* organizations—the Indigenous and Campesino State Council of Chiapas (CEOIC)" (Burguete, 1995, p. 12). Furthermore, FIPI-Mexico put out a plea for transnational indigenous organizations to come to Chiapas and act as human-rights observers while the military conducted its January 1994 campaign. CONIC "responded immediately by organizing international delegations which traveled to the battle zones" (Cleaver, 1994b).

The above is only a partial listing, for one issue area. A full listing of all NGOs for all issue areas would run for pages. Tables 1–4 highlight the names of NGOs that were prominent in several issue areas during 1994.

Acting in tandem with these organizations were the second type: the network-facilitating and infrastructure-building NGOs. These are not defined by specific issues; rather, they assist other NGOs and activists, no matter the issue. They specialize in facilitating communications, organizing demonstrations, caravans and other events, and fostering education and exchange activities. See Table 5 for a list of some prominent examples.

Of these, the most important from a technological and training standpoint is the Association for Progressive Communications (APC), a global network of computer networks that has many affiliates, such as the U.S.-based Peacenet and Conflictnet, and the nascent La Neta in Mexico. All are attached or have access to the Internet. The APC and its affiliates amount to a worldwide computer-conferencing and e-mail system for activist NGOs. It enables them to consult and co-ordinate, disseminate news and other information, and put pressure on governments, including by mounting fax-writing and e-mail campaigns. The APC also helps activist NGOs to acquire the equipment and the training their members may need in order to get on-line.[15]

Of course, using the Internet to accomplish all this depends on there being good telecommunications systems for making Internet connections. In Mexico, such systems—including APC affiliates like La Neta, which came weakly on-line in 1993, as well as direct connections available only at universities or through a few commercial providers, many of which are expensive for activists—were pretty reliable in Mexico City, other major cities, and at universities. Connecting to the Internet from a place like San Cristóbal de las Casas is another story; it can be done, but only at slow speeds and not very reliably. Faxes and telephone calls afford better communications.[16]

The APC itself did not have activists in Mexico specifically because of Chiapas, but other important infrastructure-building NGOs did. These included an American NGO, Global Exchange; a Canadian networking NGO, Action Canada; and Mexico's CONPAZ (see Table 5). Again, cooperative connections existed among all such organizations. (At the same time, it should be noted that issue-oriented NGOs also serve as disseminators of information to other NGOs. One of the most important and reliable has been the "Miguel Agustín

---

[15]For general background, see Frederick (1993a).

[16]The notion that Marcos uploads his statements to the Internet is apocryphal. He does reportedly have a laptop computer with him in the jungle, but uploading and downloading anything is accomplished by having diskettes taken to San Cristóbal.

Pro" Center for Human Rights, which issues daily and weekly bulletins.)

Few transnational NGOs had or would install a permanent presence in Chiapas—a key exception was Global Exchange (not to mention some IGOs, like the International Red Cross). Most had representatives who would come and go episodically, with their timing often depending on meetings organized by the EZLN, activities organized by other NGOs, or on their own plans to visit and draw up a report. Nonetheless, the new communications technologies enabled many NGOs to maintain a "virtual presence" by being on mailing lists of supporters, signing petitions, participating in fax- and letter-writing campaigns, and circulating NGO-derived reports on the Internet and in other media. Such a "virtual presence" may be important to the conduct of a transnational social netwar.

Throughout, the fact that the Catholic Church, especially the diocese at San Cristóbal and church-related Mexican NGOs like the "Fray Bartolome de las Casas" Center for Human Rights, had a strong presence in Chiapas was crucial for the whole array of NGOs discussed above. The diocese and the NGOs related to it, soon to include CONPAZ, provided a physical point of contact—a key node—for the transnational activists. (Such a node is missing in other states, like Guerrero and Oaxaca, where new conflicts are emerging.)

Addressing Tensions, Gaining Confidence

Thus the Zapatista networking conformed to what we would expect from the analytic background presented earlier in this study. The activists' networking assumed informal, often ad hoc shapes. Participation shifted constantly, depending partly on the issues—though some NGOs did maintain a steady involvement and sought, or were accorded, leading roles. While the NGOs generally seemed interested in the collective growth of the networks, to create what would later be termed a "network of struggles," each still aimed to preserve its autonomy and independence and had its own particular interests and strategies in mind. Clearly, the NGOs were—and are still—learning how to use this new approach to strategy, which requires that they develop and sustain a shared identity as a network and stress information operations.

There was impressive solidarity and harmony when a swarm took shape around a hot issue, such as demanding a halt to military operations or pressing for the release of an imprisoned Zapatista. At the same time, there was never complete solidarity and harmony among all members of the Zapatista networks at all times. According to our interviews, coordination was not always smooth. Problems and differences would get worked out most readily among activists present in the conflict zone, but the tone of debate might be quite different and more contentious in Mexico City. Indeed, some significant tensions existed, and surfaced, that had limiting effects.

For example, the EZLN's initial rhetoric in January 1994 was quite socialist in style and content, and it barely acknowledged the importance of *indigenista* issues like cultural rights and autonomy. In February, following Marcos's lead, a rebalancing occurred: the socialist rhetoric diminished, and demands for attention to indigenous rights came to the fore (see Van Cott, 1996, pp. 74–77; Nash, 1995). This reassured many indigenous-rights NGOs that were already supporting the EZLN. Yet some, like FIPI, wanted to see even more Indian and less Marxist language used, and wanted the EZLN to join in building a pan-Indian movement—but the EZLN remained determined to keep its goals in a nationalist framework. From another perspective, some leftist activists were not comfortable with the EZLN's elevation of ethnicity as a factor; the Marxist left in particular regards economic class as the key factor, and ethnicity as a divisive rather than unifying factor, in social struggles.

Overall, however, many Mexican NGO activists gained confidence in their turn to networked approaches to communication, coordination, and mobilization, in regard not only to the conflict in Chiapas but also to other efforts to promote reform in Mexico. As Sergio Aguayo remarked (as a leader of Civic Alliance, a multi-NGO pro-democracy network that was created to monitor the August 1994 presidential election and later chosen in August 1995 by the EZLN to conduct a national poll, known as the National Consultation, about opinions of the EZLN):[17] "We're seeing a profound effect on their [the NGOs'] self-esteem. They've proven to themselves that they can

---

[17]Sergio Aguayo has been one of the keenest analysts of the rise of NGOs in Mexico. For example, see Sergio Aguayo Quezada, "Los modos del Marcos," *La Jornada*, January 10, 1996, as received via Internet e-mail list.

coordinate and do difficult tasks which have significant political implications."[18] Furthermore, "If civic organizations have had so much impact, it is because they created networks and because they have received the support and solidarity of groups in the United States, Canada, and Europe."[19]

Meanwhile, Mexican NGOs gained a high approval rating among the public. In an opinion poll for the magazine *Este País*, 67 percent of the respondents claimed not to have faith in the judicial system, and only 20 percent said they had faith in the government institutions. In contrast, NGOs garnered an 80 percent credibility rating (Scott, 1995).

Table 1

Human-Rights NGOs

TRANSNATIONAL
    Amnesty International
    International Commission of Jurists
    Physicians for Human Rights
AMERICAN
    Americas Watch
    Minnesota Advocates for Human Rights
CANADIAN
    Inter-Church Committee on Human Rights in Latin America
    La Ligue de Droit et Libertes
MEXICAN
    Mexican Academy of Human Rights
    Mexican National Network of Civil Human Rights Organizations

---

[18]As quoted in Scott (1995), as posted on the Internet.

[19]From Sergio Aguayo, "Citizens Chip Away at the Dinosaur," *Los Angeles Times*, August 15, 1996, p. B9.

Table 2

Ecumenical NGOs

TRANSNATIONAL
  Jesuit Refugee Service
AMERICAN
  Pastors for Peace
  Fellowship of Reconciliation (FOR)
CANADIAN
  Inter-Church Committee on Human Rights in Latin America (ICCHRLA)
MEXICAN
  Catholic Bishops of Chiapas
  Center for Human Rights "Fray Bartolome de las Casas"

Table 3

Indigenous-Rights NGOs

TRANSNATIONAL
  Continental Coordinating Commission of Indigenous Nations (CONIC)
  International Indigenous Treaty Council (IITC)
AMERICAN
  South and Mesoamerican Indian Information Center (SAIIC)
CANADIAN
  Okanaga Nation
MEXICAN
  State Coalition of Indigenous and Campesino Organizations (CEOIC)
  Coordinator of Mayan Organizations Struggling for Liberation (COLPUMALI)

Table 4

Trade and Development NGOs

AMERICAN
  Institute for Agriculture and Trade Policy (IATP)
  Food First
MEXICAN
  Red Mexicana de Accion Frente al Libre Comercio (RMALC)

Table 5

Infrastructure-Building and Network-Facilitating NGOs

TRANSNATIONAL
    Association for Progressive Communications (APC)
    Peacenet
    Conflictnet

AMERICAN
    Global Exchange
    International Action Center
    InterHemispheric Education Resource Center

CANADIAN
    Action Canada Network
    Mexican Solidarity Network

MEXICAN
    Coalition of Nongovernmental Organizations for Peace (CONPAZ)

Chapter Five

TRANSFORMATION OF THE CONFLICT

The physical—and electronic—swarming of activist NGOs into Mexico rapidly transformed the context and conduct of the Zapatista conflict. Within days, a traditional guerrilla insurgency changed into an information-age social netwar. The principal participants already had, or had shifted in the direction of, networked organizational structures—a point that is much truer for the EZLN and its NGO cohorts than for the Mexican government and army, but applies to the latter as well.

Within weeks, if not days, the conflict became less about "the EZLN" than about "the Zapatista movement" writ large, which, as elucidated in Chapters Three and Four, included a swarm of NGOs. This movement, as befits the analytic background in Chapter Two, had no precise definition, no clear boundaries. To some extent, it had centers of activity for everything from the discussion of issues to the organization of protest demonstrations, notably San Cristóbal de las Casas and Mexico City. It had organizational centers where issues got raised before being broadcast, such as the diocese in San Cristóbal and CONPAZ. And it drew on a core set of NGOs, e.g., the ones in Tables 1–5 at the end of Chapter Four. Yet it had no formal organization, or headquarters, or leadership, or decisionmaking body. The movement's membership (assuming it can be called that) was generally ad hoc and in flux; it could shift from issue to issue and from situation to situation, partly depending on which NGOs had representatives physically visiting the scene at the time, which NGOs were mobilizable from afar and how (including electronically), and what issues were involved. Evidently, some NGOs took a constant interest in the Zapatista movement; others showed solidarity only episodically, especially if it was not high up on their agenda of concerns. In short, the Zapatista movement writ large was a sprawling, swirling, amorphous collectivity—and in a sense, its indefinition was part of its strength.[1]

ZAPATISTA EMPHASIS ON "INFORMATION OPERATIONS"

As "information operations" came to the fore, the insurgents further decentralized organizationally and deemphasized combat operations in favor of gaining tighter links with the NGOs. Meanwhile, the latter utilized, and advocated that others utilize, nonviolent strategies for using varied new and old media to pressure the Mexican government to rein in its military response and accede to negotiations.

After twelve days of hard, sometimes brutal fighting in January, the government did indeed halt its initial counteroffensive. Since Mexican military forces were proving quite effective against the Zapatistas, the government's forbearance remains a puzzle. The cessation of combat operations cannot be explained by traditional state-centered theories wherein, for example, it might be thought that fear of recrimination from the U.S. government would constrain Mexican behavior. In this case, there was no overt U.S. support for the suppression of the EZLN, though there may have been some tacit or indirect support. Despite tacit external support from other governments, the Mexican government found itself unable to deflect the initiatives of the EZLN and the NGOs.

As the netwar developed, it actually impelled two Mexican presidents to halt combat operations and turn to political dialogue and negotiations: The first, as noted above, was President Salinas in January 1994, after which negotiations took place at the main cathedral in San Cristóbal de las Casas. Then a year later, in February 1995, his successor, President Ernesto Zedillo (1994–2000), four days after ordering the army to expand its presence in the conflict zone and go arrest the EZLN's leaders, called a halt and agreed to a new round of negotiations, now at San Andrés Larráinzar. Both turns of events surprised government officials, army officers, and the public at large.

---

[1]The literature available on the Zapatista movement so far simply does not provide for a precise definition of "the Zapatista movement."

The halt in January 1994 also came as a surprise to the EZLN, whose leaders expected to wage war for months before seeing any possibility of negotiations. The government even agreed to treat the EZLN's home base in the rain forest as a "free zone" essentially under the EZLN's own rule, for the time being.

What led President Salinas, and later Zedillo, to halt military operations and agree to dialogue and negotiations? Varied propositions have been raised for explaining their decisions: e.g., confidence that the army had gained the upper hand, or worries about a backlash among foreign creditors and investors, damage to Mexico's image in the media, infighting among Mexico's leaders, or a widespread aversion to violence among the Mexican public. Our analysis, however, is that in both instances, the transnational activist netwar—particularly the information operations stemming from it—was a key contributing factor. It lay behind many of the other explanations, including arousing media attention and alarming foreign investors. This activism was made possible by networking capabilities that had emerged only recently as a result of the information revolution. In this conflict, "global civil society" proved itself for the first time as a key new actor in relations between states and vis-à-vis other non-state actors. The NGOs were able to accomplish this because of their information operations. Mexican officials admit that they were overwhelmed by the "information war" in the early days of the conflict.

These transformations in the character of the war are reflected in changes in the war aims of the contending sides. The EZLN and its NGO allies quickly moved to advocate radical reform rather than revolution and overthrow of the government. At the same time, the EZLN avoided seeking ties to Mexico's opposition political parties; at times, in the months ahead, it would even spurn the key leftist party, the Democratic Revolutionary Party (PRD). The government's aims exhibited a similarly moderated approach to crisis resolution, built on notions of containing the uprising locally and accommodating the EZLN's least threatening demands. This was a far cry from the dynamics in traditional guerrilla war, where the aims are often the overthrow of the government on the one hand, and the crushing of revolt on the other.

As the NGOs swarmed into Mexico, the EZLN proved entirely receptive to their role, and the artful Subcomandante Marcos clarified that a new model of social conflict and transformation was emerging. He had long been interested in the "power of the word."[2] Now, he and other EZLN leaders claimed to eschew Leninist, Maoist, and Fidelista models in which an army or party must seize power as the vanguard of a socialist revolution. Instead, the EZLN's agenda (e.g., political democracy, local autonomy) began to sound more reformist than revolutionary (see Castañeda, 1995). Marcos denied that the EZLN wanted to conquer the state (though it aimed to change the state), and he proclaimed a key role for civil-society actors in the EZLN's vision of the conflict:

> We do not want state power. It is civil society that must transform Mexico—we are only a small part of that civil society, the armed part—our role is to be the guarantors of the political space that civil society needs.[3]

In this emergent doctrine, the mobilization of civil society—not the expansion of the insurgent army—became the key strategic element. Indeed, once the fighting ended and negotiations commenced, in March 1994 Marcos emphasized his expectation that

> war will be exorcised by the pressure put on by civil society throughout the country to fulfill the agreements. . . . The problem will arise if civil society becomes exhausted, tired, collapses; in that case every thing will be left loose and then they will jump on us through the military route.[4]

This was not just disingenuous tactical rhetoric from Marcos. He had given considerable thought to it as a doctrine and strategy. Moreover, as discussed earlier, many activist NGOs were already aligned

---

[2]*El Poder de la Palabra* was the title of the master's thesis written in 1980 by the man alleged to be Marcos, namely Rafael Sebastian Guillen Vicente.

[3]From a videotaped interview with Subcommandante Marcos, as reported and footnoted in an editorial by Peter Rosset, "Insurgent Mexico and the Global South: A New Kind of Guerrilla Movement?" in *Food First News and Views,* newsletter of the Institute for Food and Development Policy, May 13, 1994, unpaginated ascii text, as circulated on the Internet.

[4]From a statement by Subcommandante Marcos, March 4, 1994, as reported by the Academia Mexicana de Derechos Humanos, *Special Bulletin Conflict in Chiapas,* Year 1, No. 8, March 1–7, 1994, Chronology, Second Part, unpaginated ascii text, as circulated on the Internet.

with this doctrinal view. Indeed, it is from their world that the ideas sprang in recent years to construct "global civil society" as a counter to state and corporate powers.[5] Nonviolent, media-oriented strategies figure strongly in this emerging doctrine.

Against this background, EZLN leaders and NGO activists turned to "information operations" to deter and counteract the government's resort to military operations. They strove to dominate the "information space" (e.g., in the media, via faxes, and on the Internet) in ways that compensated for the EZLN's inability to hold much physical territory or to project power outside Chiapas on its own. Some methods (e.g., publicity-generating caravans, fax-writing campaigns) were noted in the earlier discussion about the mobilization right after the insurrection. Since then, ever more diverse ways of conducting information operations have appeared. We identify and discuss a few in the next paragraphs.

The NGOs can claim, correctly, that they maintained a strong, visible presence that helped prevent violence and promote negotiations. A symbolic highlight in early 1994 was their presence in the "Three Rings of Peace" that surrounded the site in San Cristóbal de las Casas of the government-EZLN negotiations. Moreover, while no Mexican (and obviously no foreign) NGO representatives sat at the government-EZLN negotiating table, they developed an influential presence via the two key commissions that functioned alongside the table, in order to help keep negotiating process on track: the Comisión de Concordia y Pacificación (COCOPA—Commission for Harmony and Reconciliation), whose members are from the Mexican congress; and especially the Comisión Nacional de Intermediación (CONAI—National Mediation Commission), which was headed by Samuel Ruíz and has other representatives from civil society. Both commissions, particularly the latter, made for a more open information environment, which made it difficult for the Mexican government to seek to put down this conflict by using traditional tools of control, cooptation, deception, and repression.

---

[5]For additional background on the idea of "global civil society," see Frederick (1993a) and Lipschutz (1992). Cleaver (1995b) is an example of a U.S. activist arguing, in regard to the Zapatista conflict, that state power is not the goal of civil-society activists. Rather, they wish to transform society so that it reflects the nonhierarchical, democratic character of the network.

The EZLN evidently aimed to prolong negotiations for as long as possible, in as public a fashion as possible. (Initially, they did this partly by playing the "*indigena* card" and talking about Mayan cosmology and the Mayan long sense of time).[6] Indeed, the EZLN and some NGOs seemed quite comfortable with the "theater" of prolonged negotiations, including the process of episodically breaking them off, or threatening to break them off, over some issue (e.g., the arrest of an alleged EZLN leader, apparent government disrespect for some EZLN position, increased army activity in Chiapas) and then renewing the negotiations (e.g., after the release of such a leader, as in the cases of Javier Elorriaga and of a man alleged to be the EZLN's top leader, Comandante Germán).[7] Social netwar involves a lot of theater.

In this vein, the EZLN and supportive NGOs worked ceaselessly to keep foreign as well as Mexican activists, observers, journalists, and intellectuals physically present in or near the conflict zone. Maintaining a physical presence there was evidently very important for this social netwar—without it, the virtual presence exercised through the Internet, fax campaigns, and the media would surely have meant little. Much of this presence consisted of highly visible observers and monitors—from their appearance, they were clearly not *indigenas*, and many carried prominent ID placards—in some villages in the conflict zone. There, they watched for, and presumably helped deter, potential human-rights abuses by troops and other actors in the zone.

More to the point, the EZLN, through Marcos, succeeded in convening several dramatic (though often argumentative and inconclusive) conferences that attracted thousands of foreign and Mexican activists to the scene. The first, in April 1994, was a National Democratic Convention, held in a newly constructed amphitheater named "Aguascalientes." Among other things, this conference broached the notion of creating a Zapatista National Liberation Front (FZLN),

---

[6]Some military officers reportedly believe that the *indigena* card has been foisted on Mexico by outsiders as a way to seek control over Mexico.

[7]The latter case was especially dramatic. After the Mexican government arrested Germán in October 1995, the activists went to work, calling for his release, and the EZLN pulled out of peace talks. This sent the Mexican stock market tumbling. The government soon released him for lack of evidence.

which was formally founded in 1997. Next, the National Consultation—a nationwide poll the EZLN conducted regarding its future options in August–September 1995 with the assistance of a Mexican NGO, the Civic Alliance—had the air of a virtual conference. Following the construction of additional "Aguascalientes" sites, the EZLN convened a Continental Encounter For Humanity and Against Neoliberalism in April 1996, and an Intercontinental Encounter for Humanity and Against Neoliberalism in August 1996. These latter two conferences were attended, or supported from afar, by various U.S. and French luminaries of the left, which helped gain the attention of global media. Next, the Second Intercontinental Encounter For Humanity and Against Neoliberalism was held in Spain in July 1997, attracting mainly European activists. Both Intercontinental Encounters were organized to a large extent via the Internet. Though no conferences have been convened in the conflict zone since 1996, the activist presence there swelled again following a massacre in Acteal in December 1997. During 1994 and 1995, the government behaved gingerly toward the foreign presence in Chiapas, partly because it attracted media coverage; but since 1996, measures have been taken to control and curtail it (as we shall discuss).

These conferences gave Marcos renown for having a "capacidad convocatoria" (convocational capacity) that attracted civil-society allies, legitimized the EZLN, and thus enabled it to break out its confinement, at least in ideational and informational senses. All this represented a radical departure from the classic guerrilla style, leading one keen observer to posit that real fighting had been superseded by a "shadow war":

> Neither the EZLN nor the government has fired a shot since the cease-fire, and no peace agreement exists. The stand-off is explained by an inescapable truth: the government cannot afford the political cost of attacking troops who repeatedly, in Marcos's communiques, offer their blood for sacrifice; the Zapatistas cannot afford the military costs of violating the cease-fire. And yet the war goes on, according to Marcos. But what kind of war? The only kind the EZLN can afford, a symbolic one, fought with communiques, bellicose gestures, and elaborately staged theatrical events. The shadow war springs from and plays on a native Mexican tradition of ritual gesture that is shared by warriors and audience alike, and with Marcos as stage manager, it has proved as effective as the blood shed in January, and Marcos's postscripts, in keeping the

Zapatistas alive for a very long year, against all the odds.
(Guillermoprieto, 1995, pp. 39–40.)

Zapatista information operations were directed at both the Mexican
government and public, and at foreign governments and publics. Of
the latter, the United States was the most salient target, but European governments were targeted as well. For a decade or two, Mexican intellectuals, scholars, critics, and activists have pointed out that
a good way to get their message known is to make a statement in
Washington, D.C., New York, or some other prominent venue in the
United States, so that it is picked up, commented on, and fed back
into Mexico by the U.S. media. This way, their message has greater
impact and is seen by more people than if they made the statement
in Mexico City. The Internet amplifies this dynamic. Information
that originates but may be downplayed or otherwise neglected in
Mexico can be sent by Mexican NGOs to U.S.-based NGOs, which
then disseminate it back into Mexico in various forms and by way of
various media, in order to compel the attention of Mexican officials.

According to our interviews, rapid access to information via the
Internet, faxes, or other means sometimes also enabled NGO representatives, especially those with offices in Washington, to lobby in
Congress and at the State Department. What is posted on the Internet or accessible through it, not to mention what gets circulated by
faxes and phone calls, can be a boon to the knowledge base of an activist, strengthening his or her hand for going into meetings not only
with other activists but also with government officials.

Thus, the new information and communications technologies help
NGOs export a conflict to foreign venues and engage influential audiences there. Seeing something on the Internet may sometimes
raise activists' expectations, unrealistically, that something will be
done about it—but at the same time, this practice can help surface
and sustain an issue that may otherwise have less visibility in distant
offices.

The Zapatistas' information operations were often aimed at government officials, but at times they were aimed at the media, to oblige it
to pay attention and render reportage. While the Mexican army
gradually regained control of much of the physical territory in Chiapas, the government never regained the kind of control it used to

have over the "infosphere." Mexico's press (notably, the newspaper *La Jornada*) showed increasing independence. When initial attempts at press blackouts were followed by complaints from NGOs and media organizations, President Salinas declared the country wide open to national and international media. The media became a key battlespace for social netwar, largely because the NGOs made it so. The government found itself seeing the NGOs as more important and more difficult to control than the media.

Many activists do not have confidence in the mainstream media; some view it, in the aggregate, as a hostile, biased, or inaccurate actor when it comes to reporting about social struggles. But they also know it to be an important actor that can be put to good use. While part of the printed press in Mexico (notably, *La Jornada*) proved open to reporting about the EZLN and its views, radio and especially television companies remained likely to reflect the government's views and to refrain from reporting on the EZLN's or the NGOs' views. This the NGOs sought to counteract. According to one Mexican activist (Reygadas, 1994, p. 83, translation),

> A strategy exists among the electronic communications media to isolate the conflict and make it disappear from news reports. Facing this, an information strategy is necessary to show how democracy and peace in the whole country are linked tightly to [achieving] a deep solution to the demands of the Zapatistas and campesinos of Chiapas.

In one early case, for example, NGOs attracted the foreign media to inquire into their postings on the Internet, and the ensuing publicity "forced Televisa, Mexico's largely state-controlled television network, to report the official demands of the guerrillas, who were able to get their side of the story across during crucial moments in the group's negotiations with the government" (Vincent, 1996).

While all parties to the conflict knew that radio, television, and the press were part of the battlespace, months passed before government officials realized the significance of the Internet—and "cyberspace" generally—for the EZLN and the NGOs. Then, in April 1995, as noted earlier, Mexico's Foreign Minister Jose Angel Gurría observed that

> Chiapas . . . is a place where there has not been a shot fired in the last fifteen months. . . . The shots lasted ten days, and ever since the war has been a war of ink, of written word, a war on the Internet.

Reflecting on this some time later, Marcos would remark philosophically (in Le Bot, 1997, p. 349, translation)[8] that

> one space . . . so new that no one thought a guerrilla could turn to it, is the information superhighway, the Internet. It was territory not occupied by anybody . . . the problem that distresses Gurría is that he has to fight against an image that he cannot control from Mexico, because the information is simultaneously on all sides.

But at the time, many activists took umbrage at Gurría's remark. It seemed denigrating. It seemed to mean that, in the government's view, this was not a real war, just a war of words. And the government did not understand that the activists were waging a "war of peace." But even if Gurría did mean to diminish the significance of the conflict, his remark is telling. It meant that the Mexican government was waking to the changing nature of conflict in the information age. During 1994, few Mexican officials had any awareness that the EZLN and sympathetic NGOs were developing a strong presence on the Internet by means of e-mail lists, computer conferencing systems, and Web pages that were often accessed by hundreds, perhaps thousands, of activists in North America and around the world. Eventually, these officials began to learn what the NGOs already knew—that a new model of conflict was emerging, one in which the use of the new information technologies reflected the rise of radically new approaches to organization, doctrine, and strategy.

While many NGO activists viewed their roles in Mexico as crucial for determining the course and conduct of the conflict in Chiapas, they also knew that their networks and information operations were not easy to sustain. Various techniques were used in this conflict to make it simple for people to join in during periods of activity. These included putting on the Internet ready-to-go "action forms" (basically, form letters) along with the fax and telephone numbers of who to send them to, enabling readers to respond to "urgent ap-

---

[8]We are indebted to Kathleen Bruhn for pointing this statement out. Le Bot's interview with Marcos dates from the summer of 1996.

peals" for support (Whaley (1995) addresses this as a general issue). During periods of inactivity, it has been noted (Cleaver, 1995b) that it is not easy for a network to keep up its morale and energy levels; one way for activists to do this is to keep reminding themselves of past information operations that helped a social movement affect government policies.

Still, even though the Internet is a boon to social activism, and though it harbors a treasure trove of postings, many activists report being wary of much of the information that comes across it on a day-to-day basis. They do not regard it as a panacea or a substitute for other forms of knowledge gathering. Some do not even view it as a key source of information, compared to what they can learn from personal contacts, fact-finding visits, or primary sources not on the Internet. Much of what gets circulated on the Internet is viewed as a voluminous barrage of mixed quality and relevance—often resulting in unreliable, skewed, junk, false, or kooky information, based on rumor, misunderstanding, or posturing. Moreover, there is concern about the Internet being used for "crying wolf" and for manipulation by people with hidden agendas.[9] Thus, many activists are selective, looking on the Internet only for reports from those few individuals and organizations they specifically trust. Some activists prefer targeted faxes (not to mention phone calls) over the wide-open Internet, and make very limited use of it. This speaks to a point made in an earlier chapter that netwar should not be reduced to, or confused with, Internet-war.

This wariness is increased by a concern that government actors may post misinformation and disinformation on the Internet in order to provoke an overreaction that embarrasses the activists. Indeed, even though deliberate misinformation and disinformation are not common, all sides accuse the others of it, and say that they have a hard time combating it. One short e-mail message posted in February 1995 remains particularly notorious. In it, a U.S. professor sounded a warning, reportedly telephoned to him by activists on the scene, that

---

[9]For example, we heard a story of a church-related group that established an open e-mail circuit to discuss refugee issues involving Guatemala. This circuit was taken over by guerrilla-related groups who used it to disseminate their own postings, including for fund-raising purposes. The church-related group has since replaced it with a closed system.

army troops were on the move, bombs were being dropped, and bodies were piling up in a hospital in a town near San Cristóbal. It urged the reader to spread the word, including by passing the e-mail on. Six months later, this highly inaccurate message was still being recirculated, appearing in discussion groups and on-line conferencing systems far removed from any specific concern with Mexico. As a result, the "Fray Bartoleme de las Casas" Center for Human Rights in San Cristóbal saw fit to post an e-mail message repudiating it. The Canadian Broadcasting Corporation (CBC) even put together a special radio program about the message and its genesis. The message was evidently written on the basis of second-hand reports and was not intended as misinformation or disinformation—but it is a good example of how that can occur anyway.

Activists have reported several possible instances of information warfare attacks against them, particularly during the 1994–1996 period. For example, La Neta went down for mysterious reasons in late 1994; and a key Internet e-mail list, Chiapas-L, was interrupted a few times over the years, again for mysterious reasons, prompting a move of its server from a site in Mexico to one in the United States. But it is acknowledged that there may have been technical or other innocent reasons for such temporary system failures. In addition, two Mexican congressional representatives once claimed that their e-mail had been tampered with. Also, a man reputed to be a Mexican military intelligence officer was allegedly behind a provocative posting on the Mexico2000 e-mail list; he was also said to have harassed a list member by sending her odd messages, and was suspected of being behind some electronic tampering with her and another activist's e-mail accounts and computer systems. Throughout this period, various activists suspected that their telephone and computer lines were monitored without being disrupted. All in all, these incidents indicate the possibilities for information-warfare measures to counter the Zapatistas. But they do not add up to much, and do not imply that a netwar could be seriously disrupted for long by disrupting activities on the Internet.

From 1994 through early 1998, offensive information warfare, as an aggressive activity conducted by computer hackers, was not a major concern for any side in the Zapatista social netwar (though it surely attracted attention the few times it occurred or was suspected). But there are indications that this may change. A faction of pro-Zapatista radicals based in New York, drawing on ideas coming out of radical theater circles and inspired by the shock tactics of Earth First! and ACT-UP, has begun to advocate "electronic civil disobedience."[10] The intent is to go beyond the electronic protest tactics (e.g., e-mail and fax campaigns) that Zapatista activists have emphasized so far, and focus on creating "virtual sit-ins" that may shut down sensitive Web sites and Internet servers in Mexico and/or the United States, in order to "disrupt the flow of normal business and governance." The protagonists of this view are trying to create software for use on anonymous offshore servers—"ping engines, spiders, and offshore spam engines"—that will enable them, and any other individual anywhere who wants to join, to conduct what amount to massive, remote-control, standoff, swarming attacks in cyberspace (see Wray, 1998a, 1998b).[11]

The prospect of this happening is not being well received by the mainstream of the Zapatista movement. And if such an effort develops, it may well have divisive effects, possibly leading to a split between those proponents of netwar (yes, they have adopted the term)[12] who believe that new, real-world organizational designs should be the basis for activist doctrines and strategies, and the more anarchistic proponents who believe that theatrical technological strikes—"digital Zapatismo"—should lie at the heart of doctrine and strategy.

---

[10]See Stefan Wray's site at http://www.nyu.edu/projects/wray/ecd.html for background and materials on electronic civil disobedience.

[11]In the words of one proponent, Stefan Wray (1998b): "Given that the hybridization of the politicized hacker and the computerized activist is still in its period of incunabula, or infancy, we can only expect that these more sophisticated tactics of ping engines, spiders, and offshore spam engines are merely signs of greater things to come. While I have been seeing these types of computerized tactics begin to emerge within the context of the global pro-Zapatista movement, there is no doubt that other radical social movements are also beginning to push the envelope and move beyond using e-mail and web sites solely for communication, but for direct action as well."

[12]We do not make a point of this until Chapter Seven, but it should be noted that the term "netwar" has been accepted, used, cited, and criticized in pro-Zapatista circles since 1994 (e.g., Simon (1995) led to a brief storm of discussion as to whether or not netwar could make Mexico "ungovernable").

ATTENUATION AND RESTRUCTURING OF COMBAT OPERATIONS

The military dimension was partly, but not entirely, submerged in this new kind of conflict. Indeed, for both the EZLN and the military, credible threats to renew the use of force remained a key aspect of strategy. After the initial period of open combat, the EZLN retreated, but it still retained some ability to return to the attack. Thus, an insurgent "army in being" emerged, one that encouraged circumspect behavior on the government's part and lent greater weight to the blandishments of the NGOs that urged nonviolent, peaceful solutions to the crisis in Chiapas. At the same time, despite (and in some ways because of) the lack of combat operations, the army developed a strategy of "blanketing" the villages of the region, in the hope that its presence would tamp down or deter any resurgence of the fighting and, at the same time, convince the EZLN that it had no significant military option and no alternative to negotiations.

Indeed, the military, though reportedly displeased at being reined in by the government, responded to changing circumstances with some adroitness. In many cases, counterguerrilla operations would generally call for keeping forces massed, for self-defense as well as to be ready for search-and-destroy missions. The Mexican army took the opposite tack, creating much smaller operational units, of roughly platoon size (36–45 troops, with an officer in command), and deploying them in a dispersed fashion across Chiapas, blanketing the state with the aim of deterring new outbreaks of fighting. In a traditional guerrilla war, this move might have had disastrous consequences,[13] inviting the defeat in detail of one isolated detachment at a time. For counternetwar, however, this scheme for decentralizing authority and deployment proved optimal, and fighting soon died out almost completely.

---

[13]In counterinsurgencies in the 1960s and 1970s, the Mexican army experimented unsuccessfully with small units and dispersed deployments. These earlier failures could be traced to organizational requirements for field-grade officers, of which there were not enough to control even small detachments, and to inadequacies in electronic communications. In operations against the EZLN, the army opted to devolve greater authority to lower-ranking officers and enjoyed much-enhanced communications and mobility, thanks in part to U.S. aid.

Meanwhile, the military's image fared poorly in this early period (see Wager and Schulz, 1995; Camp, 1997). The army resented having its field operations halted in January 1994, and again in February 1995. This, in turn, led to criticism of civilian leaders from within the armed forces (notably of Manuel Camacho, who led the government's negotiating commission and was willing to consider a broad agenda). It also led to a growing concern about the army's image. The army resented being blamed retrospectively for intelligence failures after the insurrection broke out, and then for human-rights abuses when it tried to restore order in a war zone. According to military historian Steve Wager (1995, p. 14),

> In one sense, the conflict in Chiapas represents a watershed of sorts for the army. Since the end of the Mexican Revolution, the army has always been viewed as an *intocable* or untouchable. However, the events in Chiapas seem to have brought an abrupt end to the army's mythical status.

The army's concern about the erosion of its image resulted mainly from scathing criticism it received for its operations during the first week of fighting in Chiapas (e.g., for the killing of hogtied, unarmed civilians). Stung by the media, the army also seemed alienated from the government, in that the latter had on two occasions ordered it to cease and desist for political reasons—at a time when military logic called for resolute offensive action to bring the uprising to a close. In this respect, the deterrent power of the NGOs lay less in their ability to change the material situation in Chiapas than in their ability to alter public perceptions as they excoriated the army and heaped opprobrium on the Mexican government.

Thus, at times the military found itself confounded on the one hand by NGO activists (and willing journalists) who mounted media campaigns to impugn its image, and on the other hand by episodic indecisiveness and oscillation from civilian leaders. Nonetheless, the army learned in 1994 that it was not prepared to deal with civil-society actors clamoring for access and information in a conflict zone. Since a social netwar is not a traditional insurgency, part of the challenge is to recognize that military roles rarely figure large in a counternetwar against social actors. Indeed, it might be said that army had more problems dealing with the NGOs than with the EZLN.

During 1994, the army steadily reasserted its dominance in the conflict zone, and by early 1995 it had proved that the EZLN was a "paper tiger" from a military standpoint (Wager, 1995). Yet, in the period ahead, it was not clear whether the greater challenge for the army was to show it could do well in the field against the EZLN from a military standpoint or to show it could defend its image throughout Mexico from a political and social standpoint. The army's role, like the conflict at large, was as much political as military. The army went from wanting to capture or kill Marcos, and resenting being restrained, to realizing that it would be bad for its image if it were the agency to arrest or eliminate him.

Indeed, a key aspect of the netwar for the military was that the "battlespace" consisted of both the operational field in Chiapas and the arena of the "infosphere." The fact that Mexico was fighting a "two-front" war, both of whose "fronts" were loosely defined, made it hard to operate actively on both at once—and, as noted above, the government opted to constrain field operations, evidently in order to deal with the other front, despite the strain this put on civil-military relations.

Meanwhile, the military decided to pursue its own set of organizational, doctrinal, and technological reforms—and many of these, though harking back to reforms that had been proposed but shelved in the 1980s, were clearly desired because of Chiapas and because of related concerns about unrest breaking out elsewhere in the country.[14] Announced in 1995, the Program of Development for the Army and Air Force, looking ahead to the next century, called for a major restructuring that would, among other things, create a new set of elite units, including new small, mobile army *comandos* (commands, not commandos) for rapid-reaction purposes and new special forces units (notably those known as *Arco Iris*—Rainbow—task groups) for armed and civic action missions throughout the country, but primarily in Chiapas and Guerrero. In addition, the plan called for changes to existing special forces; the improvement of logistics (another problem for the army in January 1994); a revamping of the military intelligence system; greater incorporation of civilians into

---

[14]Some background appears in Camp (1997). Radu (1997) holds that Mexico lacks a coherent counterinsurgency doctrine or strategy.

defense activities; the acquisition of an information-warfare capability; and a rethinking and redefinition of the concept of national security. Of all these changes, the most visible and immediately effective was the creation in 1995 of the Rainbow units, which led to about 10,000 soldiers being assigned to Chiapas and elsewhere, either to replace or reinforce existing units. Though obliged to halt its offensive in February 1995, the army continued to gain ground that year by saturating the conflict zone with small detachments, many of them Rainbow units.

Thus, the netwar has had a positive side for the military. It has prompted tactical decentralization, institutional redesign in favor of smaller, more specialized and mobile forces, new efforts at joint operations, and improvements in interservice intelligence sharing. These shifts engendered some intra- and interservice tensions; but the benefits of reorganization should outweigh the difficulties and costs, in terms of an increase in military efficiency. If fully implemented, this program would amount to a "revolution within the army."[15]

The first major effect was the move to decentralize the command and control of tactical operations. Field units became smaller, with companies, and even platoons, forming into more numerous detachments somewhat larger than squad size. This shift created many more maneuver units, allowing the army to pursue its new "blanketing" strategy that was designed to prevent the outbreak of further fighting, to impede the movement of EZLN forces, and to contain them in a very limited zone.[16] Improved communication equipment and links in the Mexican army helped enable the move to smaller units.

Such decentralization, which engenders a high degree of operational latitude, carries the risk that the troops, if engaged, may overstep,

---

[15]Quote from a statement by Roderic Camp, *El Financiero*, 25 September, 1997, as posted on the Internet.

[16]In many respects, the Mexican military's approach resembles that taken by the U.S. Army and Marines in their war against the Seminoles in Florida during the mid-19th century. In this case, too, a substantial decentralization of authority and deployment took place (Mahon, 1992). This approach also resembles the multitude of small garrisons that the French established during the Algerian counterinsurgency (1954–1962), in what was called *quadrillage*.

either taking undue risks or committing unacceptable acts.[17] In Chiapas, however, a different outcome has emerged; the army's hold has deepened through dispersion and decentralization. This occurred partly because the new freedom of action ceded to tactical commanders was tempered by restrictive rules of engagement. Moreover, almost all troops deployed to Chiapas in small detachments received additional training that made them "special"—if not by U.S. elite standards, at least relative to the rest of the Mexican military.

In regard to civil-military relations, the relative circumspection and constraint with which the army behaved gives evidence of a reaffirmation of civilian control over the military. The army eagerly wanted to crush the rebellion forcefully, continuing along the lines it had established in the opening two weeks of the conflict. Yet the army complied with the government's decision to take a less violent approach that relegated the army to a "presence" mission. However, this created some intra- and interservice dissensions. Within the army, factions divided over whether it should be used in such fashion. Moreover, the army's new role and mission in Chiapas required much more intelligence; seeking the assets to support this function led the army to butt heads with other services, principally the navy, over the control and use of intelligence equipment and operators.

The netwar has obliged the army to devote much increased attention to public affairs, psychological operations, relations with NGOs, and human-rights issues. The army's concerns about generating sufficient information to do its job is but a part of a general movement to give more attention to the development of an "information strategy." This new focus has entailed efforts to cultivate better relations with the media and has extended to mounting a number of psychological operations, including "sky shouting" from helicopters with bullhorns, as well as leafleting. More importantly, the pursuit of an integrated information strategy spurred the Mexican government to form a joint intelligence apparatus that is supposed to put an end to the proprietary, baronial practices that have characterized its competing intelligence organizations throughout the 20th century. Above all,

---

[17]In Algeria, French forces did both, which contributed to the unraveling of French policy (see Furniss, 1964; Meisel, 1962; Henissart, 1970; and Paret, 1964).

the information strategy is being keyed to a need to show respect for human rights.

All this suggests that the Mexican military has gained reasons for wanting better ties with the U.S. military—and these have materialized in a range of arms transfers, training, and education areas. One noteworthy area involves Mexico's Airborne Special Forces Groups (GAFEs), which since 1996 have been undergoing training at Fort Bragg in the United States. These special forces units are similar to U.S. Delta teams and the German *Grenzschutzgruppe-9*, in that they operate as small, mobile, dispersed, internetted teams, are trained for quick-strike operations under all manner of conditions, particularly against terrorists, do not fall under the usual chain of command, and can take tactical initiatives.[18] In Mexico's case, the GAFEs fall under the president's office rather than the secretary of defense. They are ostensibly trained and deployed for counternarcotics operations, but they have also gained counterinsurgency, antiterrorist, and other internal security roles—as evidenced by the sight of GAFEs manning roadblocks and conducting searches around Acteal right after the massacre. The creation and expansion of the GAFEs may make sense from a variety of perspectives, including counternetwar; but in today's Mexico, there appears to be some risk that they could conduct themselves in heavy-handed ways that produce human-rights and other abuses–and this may not be conducive to the calming of a social netwar.

GOVERNMENT EFFORTS AT COUNTERNETWAR

The prospects for netwar—and counternetwar—revolve around a small string of propositions about networks-versus-hierarchies, as discussed earlier: Accordingly, it can be said that hierarchies have difficulty fighting networks. It takes networks to fight networks—indeed, a government hierarchy may have to organize its own networks in order to prevail against networked adversaries. Whoever masters the network form should gain major advantages in the information age.

---

[18]See Kelly (1989, pp. 51–57) for a discussion of the German design.

By implication, a government needs agility and adaptability to cope with netwar-related threats and challenges. Counternetwar may require the development of very effective interagency mechanisms and operations, since the interagency arena is where networking may best occur in the government world. Improving civil-military, interservice, and intramilitary coordination and cooperation become essential tasks

How well do these propositions apply in Mexico's case? To assure that social and other netwars do not jeopardize Mexico's stability or reform processes, the government must improve its ability to conduct counternetwar.[19] The Zapatista case confirms that hierarchies—like the government, army, and PRI—have difficulty dealing with a networked actor (or set of actors). The case also shows that the government adapted by organizing interagency and other intergovernmental networks to try to prevail against the pro-Zapatista networks. Although the government and the army initially responded in a traditional, heavy-handed manner to the EZLN's insurrection, they have not responded idly or unthinkingly since then to this seminal case of social netwar.

Research is lacking at this time to substantiate how well they have adapted, what they have learned, and how much they have achieved. But a few developments are known. Once negotiations got under way and Chiapas was defined as more a political than a military problem, the Ministry of Government (Gobernación) took charge of overall strategy, leaving the Ministry of Defense (SEDENA) to focus on avoiding further damage to its image. An innovative interagency group was established in January 1994 at the Center for National Security and Investigation (CISEN), which fits under Gobernación and is the key agency for national security and intelligence matters.[20] This interagency group included not only CISEN but also represen-

---

[19]We remind the reader, again, that in our view this does not necessarily mean squelching a social netwar. A social netwar may have some positive effects and implications for spurring democratic reforms. The improvement of counternetwar should occur with that in mind.

[20]This step was an innovation for CISEN. But it was not the first such interagency group formed to address a national security matter. An earlier case involved Mexico's concerns in the 1980s about spillover effects from the Guatemalan insurgency, counterinsurgency, and related refugee flows along the Guatemalan border.

tatives from the ministries of national defense, social development, and several others, as well as the office of the governor of Chiapas.

The group worked to define overall government strategy toward the EZLN and related problems in Chiapas. It soon assessed that the EZLN was not a powerful force in military terms, and that the threat of other armed groups arising around the country was overstated. The strategy it developed during 1994 aimed to localize and limit the conflict, and had essentially three prongs: a military prong to keep the EZLN confined in the conflict zone, while avoiding combat and improving the army's human-rights behavior; a political prong to keep the dialogue and its agenda from becoming national in scope, and to regain control of information; and an economic prong to offer resources and mount programs that would appeal to some of the local population's needs. The strategy was also designed to let the Zapatistas talk (and let them know that there was no alternative to talking), while working gradually to diminish international attention to the EZLN and whittle down its demands. But when the EZLN's own information operations, including the media coverage of a small military operation where the EZLN broke out of its zone in December 1994, appeared to result in damage to the value of Mexico's currency and stock market that month, the interagency group saw merit in having the government resume the military offensive in early 1995.

Preliminary research indicates that federal oversight did not fare well with regard to either interservice coordination in the military or federal-state-local coordination in Chiapas. The former ran into differing bureaucratic cultures that work against information sharing and coordination among the service branches. The latter ran into the fact that the power structures in Chiapas include a network of landlords, ranchers, *caciques*, and private paramilitary forces whose modus operandi is essentially feudal, and whose interests may lie in limiting federal efforts to modernize the region, in opposing if not sabotaging federal programs that favor the *indigenas*, and in repressing the EZLN and its *indigena* supporters.[21] Some ranchers in

---

[21]This is an interesting aspect of the whole story, but we did not explore it much. There are reports, mostly from activists, that Lyndon LaRouche's organization was providing material support and ideological guidance to already well-established paramilitary forces in Chiapas. It has been sending books, articles, pamphlets, even

Chiapas were reportedly so angry at the halt of army operations against the EZLN in January 1994 that they threatened to persist with their own paramilitary operations (Reding, 1994, p. 22). How to view—and whether to restrain or unleash—such ranchers and their paramilitary forces remained an important question for federal intelligence gathering and assessment during 1994–1996. Meanwhile, officials in Mexico City realized that the varied civilian and military agencies concerned with intelligence should not be working in isolation, and that Mexico needed a "national intelligence community." But they also realized that Mexico lacked a sound "culture" for thinking about and collecting intelligence about security matters, broadly defined. Events in Chiapas brought these concerns to the fore.

In sum, beginning in 1994 the federal government, its national security apparatus, and the military had to try to transform themselves to respond to this social netwar. Yet this transformation has never been complete, and there has been a constant tension and interplay between, on the one hand, learning to treat the Zapatista movement as an information-age social netwar and, on the other hand, wanting to treat it as a traditional insurgency. The key touchstone as to which hand of strategy was prevailing was not the military—its presence and strength grew throughout, leaving the conflict zone thoroughly blanketed and penetrated by small detachments. Rather, the touchstones were, apparently, two forces over which the government had marginal control but which it knew were key players in the overall game and dearly wanted to control: the foreign NGOs and the local paramilitary forces.[22] Which hand of Mexican strategy was stronger seems to have varied mainly according to the degree of foreign NGO and media attention. When it was high, the case mainly during 1994–1996, the government seemed to understand it was caught in an information-age conflict—recall Gurría's comment. But when NGO and media attention wavered or diminished, often the case in 1997, paramilitary organizations like "Peace and Justice" grew in strength and extended their presence in areas lying around the

---

e-mail, arguing that U.S. and international capitalist organizations like the International Monetary Fund (IMF) are trying to destabilize Latin America.

[22]We caution the reader that we lack data on government decisionmaking about much of the conflict in Chiapas, and particularly about the roles of paramilitary forces. Thus many of our points here should be read as speculative rather than definitive.

conflict zone, making more likely a reversion to the heavy-handed counterinsurgency measures of an earlier generation.

This helps explain the December 1997 incident in Acteal, where, for a mixture of reasons, local paramilitary gunmen loosely affiliated with the PRI massacred a number of villagers, some of whom were EZLN sympathizers. This occurred in a period when NGO activism, and thus the Zapatista social netwar, seemed to be in abeyance and the area was returning to traditional dynamics, which favored paramilitarism. One result was an even heavier increase in the army's patrolling. But another result, once again, was the reactivation of the NGOs and their efforts at media-intensive netwar.

Dealing with civil-society NGOs—whether as allies, as in humanitarian and relief operations, or as antagonists, as in cases of human-rights and environmental abuse—is a new frontier for government officials and military officers around the world. In this case of social netwar, the Mexican government and military have longed to constrain the NGOs and other agents of social activism (e.g., some foreign Catholic priests). Even so, during much of 1994–1995 the government was quite tolerant of their presence. Surely, few other governments would have been so tolerant of such an unusual, heavy, albeit episodic influx of foreigners showing great interest in an internal security matter. During 1996, however, and especially during the international encounters that attracted thousands to Chiapas, government agents began stepped-up efforts to videotape, warn, and question foreign activists, especially those who were traveling on tourist visas but seemed engaged in activism, not tourism, and lacked affiliation with recognized NGOs. Some were deported.

This tactic was redoubled in 1997 and again in early 1998 in the aftermath of the Acteal massacre. Over 200 activists have been obliged to leave Mexico since January 1997. In one incident in April 1998, about a dozen foreigners, who were present at a site that was in the process of declaring itself an "autonomous municipality" aligned with the EZLN, were detained, interrogated, and forced to leave Mexico. In the media stir that followed, the state governor averred that "There is proof positive that they broke the law. That they were politically active, that they are destabilizing Chiapas. And neither

Mexico nor Germany nor France nor the United States can allow that."[23] In the name of nationalism, and citing constitutional proscriptions against foreigners meddling in internal politics, the government is taking a much harder line than before toward foreign activists, even though officials also point out that hundreds of special visas granting observer status have been provided to NGO representatives who have been visiting and monitoring conditions in the conflict zone.

---

[23]From Martin Roberts, "Mexican Governor Defends Expulsion of Foreigners," Reuters, April 15, 1998—as posted on the Internet.

Chapter Six

THE NETWAR SIMMERS—AND DIFFUSES

SITUATIONAL STANDOFF

In short, the netwar had its heyday in Mexico in 1994 and 1995. And except for the large international conferences convened by the EZLN in 1996, it has not fared well since then, except in episodes. During 1996, the off-and-on negotiations that the government and the EZLN began holding in 1995 at San Andrés Larráinzar ground to a halt. An agreement in February 1996 about indigenous culture and rights was supposed to be followed by additional agreements on political and economic issues. But in mid-1996, following the sentencing of its imprisoned colleague Javier Elorriaga, the EZLN withdrew from the talks. A new round of netwar activism pled for his release, which succeeded in June and set the stage for a restart of the talks. Meanwhile, however, it became clear that Mexico's executive did not want to approve what the EZLN wanted under the first agreement: local autonomy for *indigena* communities, including over natural resources.[1] Then, in September 1996, Marcos declared an indefinite suspension of the EZLN's participation in negotiations. His rationale objected to the military's growing presence in Chiapas, but he also indicated that the EZLN wanted a pause to assess the implications of the rise of the Popular Revolutionary Army (EPR—see below). At this writing, negotiations have not been resumed, though there is new talk of doing so soon.

---

[1] The government's view of the natural resources point is complicated by the prospect of new hydrocarbon deposits in Chiapas.

Ever since 1995, the military situation has remained adverse for the EZLN. The army has confined it to a small zone in Chiapas, from which it broke out only once, briefly (December 1994). The saturation/blanketing strategy has worked, including by avoiding new combat. The army is well positioned to assault and defeat the EZLN in its home base, though this remains politically inadvisable because of the transnational netwar dimensions. Indeed, the EZLN appears to have grown weaker as a military force since 1995. Some of its partisans may prefer to accept government offers of local assistance programs that the EZLN leadership rejects, while other partisans who prefer armed struggle may have left to affiliate with the EPR.

The EZLN has tried to extend its reach outside this zone, partly by sponsoring the international conferences discussed in Chapter Five, and more recently by urging other *indigena* villages in Chiapas and elsewhere to declare themselves "autonomous local governments," so that they stand free from federal, state, and PRI controls but may still demand benefits from belonging to the Mexican union. This effort, if successful, could result in peppering Chiapas and some other states with a sprawling, dispersed network of liberated zones. But it is not an effort that has proceeded very far yet (several dozen places have joined the autonomy movement), and the government is bound to resist it.

Meanwhile, since 1996, much of the Mexican public has tired of the Zapatista story and begun to doubt that it benefits Mexico, even though it has raised important reform issues. In addition, many Mexican NGO activists increasingly began to view the conflict in Chiapas as a small part, even a sideshow, in a bigger, broader game of efforts to make Mexico more democratic. Thus, the Zapatista movement receded as a matter of daily significance in Mexico in 1996 and 1997. In October 1996, the EZLN sought to break out of its confinement by sending a delegation to attend a National Indigenous Conference in Mexico City—but the government threatened to arrest any guerrillas who left the EZLN's zone in Chiapas.[2]   In

---

[2]One outcome of this was a "Cyberspace March," a campaign of sending faxes and e-mails to government, media, and NGO addresses, in order to pressure the government to allow EZLN representatives to leave Chiapas to attend the National Indigenous Conference in Mexico City. According to the government, this would be illegal

September 1997, however, 1,111 EZLN supporters, including NGO allies, did engage in a march from Chiapas to Mexico City for a rally—again, to no major public effect. It took the resurgence of old-style violence in Acteal in December 1997 to remobilize the netwar's activist partisans in Mexico and abroad, who once again used information operations to try to constrain military and paramilitary moves against the EZLN.

More to the point, Marcos and the EZLN have slowly lost the command of reform issues that they enjoyed in 1994, when their insurrection raised consciousness all over Mexico that the country was making insufficient progress toward political democracy and that many poor people were suffering adverse effects from economic liberalization. Today, however, other actors, many of them representing established opposition parties and civil-society organizations, have resumed the lead in promoting political and economic reforms and in calling for the strengthening of civil society. The main reform issue still in the hands of Marcos and the EZLN is respect for indigenous rights, including cultural and political autonomy.[3] This resonates well with *indigena* groups; and many Mexican human-rights NGOs now give indigenous issues more heed than they used to (Acosta, 1997). Nonetheless, these issues have limited appeal in the urban, economically more advanced parts of Mexico.

All actors are maneuvering against this background. Both the EZLN and the government continue to have incentives to draw the conflict out, including through the episodic theater of prolonged negotiations, in part because each evidently believes that "time" is ultimately on its side. That this was part of the EZLN's strategy seemed clear in 1994 and 1995. By 1996, it had become part of the government's strategy as well. Today, with the public's and the media's attention

---

under terms of the "Law for Dialogue and Reconciliation and a Dignified Peace in Chiapas," which was passed by the Mexican congress in 1995 to regulate the process of negotiations. The government insisted, again, that the EZLN convert fully from a military into a political movement before it would be allowed freedom of access outside the conflict zone. Nonetheless, as a result of wrangling involving COCOPA and CONAI, an ill, woman leader of the EZLN, Comandante Ramona, was allowed to attend the conference. Data are lacking, but it appears that the "Cyberspace March" had little or nothing to do with this outcome; yet it provided another activity whereby a small number of activists and sympathizers scattered around the world could express their solidarity from a distance.

[3]Diaz-Polanco (1997) provides a good overview of the autonomy issue and its variants.

flagging, with the army in a strong position in Chiapas, and with the transnational NGOs somewhat on the defensive, the government appears to be doing fairly well with its strategy.

Table 6 summarizes the chronology of this conflict through early 1998. Details for the 1994–1996 period, when the netwar was at its height, are given in Appendix A.

However, this netwar is far from over—it continues to simmer and pulsate. The conflict zone in Chiapas, and relations between the EZLN and the government, remain in conditions that are neither war nor peace, neither just military nor just political in nature. The fact that Marcos and the EZLN claim that they do not seek to seize state power, as would a traditional armed movement, takes the edge off their ambitions, making them seem less threatening. But their campaign to get *indigena* communities all over Mexico to declare their autonomy represents, in its own way, a strategy to seize power around the periphery of the state and the ruling PRI party—and that is viewed in Mexico City as potentially quite threatening.

Meanwhile, the dynamics of netwar have diffused to other areas of Mexico and beyond. In 1996 in the state of Guerrero, for example, it diffused first as social netwar with the removal of the governor, following a violent suppression of peasant protesters that aroused the wrath of human-rights NGOs, particularly after a videotape of the incident became public. Then, it diffused as a guerrilla netwar with the emergence of the EPR in Guerrero and elsewhere, an unwelcome development for the EZLN that is discussed next. Meanwhile, the Zapatistas tried to diffuse their netwar onto the global stage by means of the "Intercontinental Encounters" in 1996 and 1997, where they called for the creation of global "networks of struggle and resistance." That effort is also discussed next.

FROM THE EZLN TO THE EPR—DIFFUSION IN MEXICO

The sudden appearance of the Popular Revolutionary Army (EPR) in Guerrero, Oaxaca, and elsewhere in June 1996, and its spate of armed assaults in July, caused all sides in the Chiapas conflict to wonder anew whose side time was on. This armed group of unclear origins and dimensions quickly proved more violent than the EZLN and more able to operate in diverse parts of Mexico, leading a Mexican scholar to compare the two organizations as follows: "The Zapatistas are a local abscess. The E.P.R. is a general infection."[4]

The differences between the EPR and EZLN are striking. Recall the three layers of the Zapatista movement (Chapter Three): The EZLN, with a prominent *Ladino* leadership, has operated in conjunction with a strong social base of *indigenas* in Chiapas and a sprawling network of Mexican and transnational NGOs. The EPR, whose leadership appears to be mainly *mestizo*, has a scattered social base in the impoverished mountain villages of Guerrero and Oaxaca. It may also have a social base in an organization that appeared in January 1996: the Broad Front for the Construction of a National Liberation Movement (FAC-MLN), which is a nationwide, network-like coalition of numerous (perhaps as many as 300) leftist groups, including radical peasant and teachers unions.[5] In contrast to the EZLN, the EPR is largely shunned by the Mexican and transnational NGOs who rallied to the EZLN's cause—and the EPR has not done much to seek the NGOs' support. In addition, the EZLN and the EPR both deny having links to each other. Overall, then, the EPR is freer than the EZLN to pursue military actions on its own initiative.

The initial political aims of the two are not all that different: Both aimed at the overthrow of the PRI-based political system and for the installation of some kind of socialist system. Of course, the EZLN's goals and methods quickly moderated, as the EPR's might if it ever opts for negotiations. But if we compare just the initial aims, the major differences are less in the overall thrust than in the details—a key point being that the EPR has been the vaguer of the two with respect to the details and far more doctrinaire when it makes long pronouncements.

The differences may derive partly from their contrasting origins. The EZLN has its origins in a Maoist group, the FLN, that believed in building a social base before it proceeded with armed actions. Indeed, the FLN spurned the tactics (e.g., kidnappings, assassinations,

---

[4]From Michael S. Serrill, "Mexico's Black Mood," *TIME International Magazine,* October 7, 1996, as posted on the Internet, quoting a statement by Rafael Segovia.

[5]Just as the EPR represents a rival to the EZLN, the FAC-MLN may have been designed as a rival to the FZLN.

Table 6

Timeline Highlights, 1994–1998

1994	
Jan	EZLN revolts, army responds; Salinas opts for cease-fire, negotiations
Feb–Mar	Camacho-led commission and EZLN negotiate in San Cristóbal de las Casas
Mar	Colosio assassinated
June	EZLN rejects negotiated accord, urges civil society to rise up
Aug	EZLN convenes National Democratic Convention in "Aguascalientes"
Aug	Zedillo wins presidential election by huge margin for PRI
Dec	Army, EZLN jockey for military position; Mexican currency crisis
1995	
Feb	Zedillo orders large military operation, then halts and proposes new talks
Feb	Multiphase talks initiated at San Andrés Larráinzar
Mar	Amnesty declared for Zapatistas
Aug–Sept	EZLN generates national opinion poll, called the National Consultation
Oct	"Germán" arrested; talks broken off; "Germán" released
Nov	Preliminary agreement reached in first phase of talks
Dec	EZLN constructs additional "Aguascalientes" gathering sites
1996	
Jan	Phase-one talks resume; EZLN issues Fourth Lacandón Declaration announcing formation of FZLN as peaceful political front
Feb	Phase-one accord (on indigenous rights) signed
Mar	Phase-two talks (on political reform) commence
Apr	Continental Encounter for Humanity and Against Neoliberalism
May	Elorriaga sentenced; peace talks at risk
June	Talks postponed; Elorriaga released
July–Aug	First Intercontinental Encounter (convened in Chiapas)
Sept	Marcos and EZLN announce indefinite suspension of negotiations

Table 6, continued

1997	
July	Second Intercontinental Encounter (convened in Spain)
Sept	EZLN representatives march to Mexico City; FZLN founded as political front
Dec	Massacre of EZLN sympathizers in Acteal by paramilitaries
1998	
Jan	Military blanketing deepens, but operations attenuated after protests
Apr	Government steps up deportations of foreign activists
Current situation (April 1998)	
	Neither war nor peace—the netwar simmers and diffuses (e.g., EPR)
	State still constrained by nonstate actors (e.g., EZLN, NGOs)
	Mexican political system remains unbalanced, though not unpopular or unstable
	Win-win, lose-lose, and win-lose outcomes all still possible in Chiapas

assaults) of most other armed groups in the 1960s and 1970s. The EPR's origins are still not clear. One story, mainly voiced by the government, is that the EPR has its principal roots in PROCUP, a murky group that claims to be Maoist but has a record of Stalinist behavior and sectarian violence.[6] PROCUP is the kind of group that the FLN would once have criticized; at times, PROCUP has even been thought to be penetrated by Mexico's security agencies. To the extent that the EPR is an offspring of PROCUP, analysts should remain dubious of its nature. The other story, averred by an EPR leader and by jour-

---

[6]Guerrero has a long history of giving rise to guerrilla groups. The two important insurgencies of the 1970s were both there: the National Civic Revolutionary Association (ANCR), led by Genaro Vasquez Rojas until his death in 1972; and the Party of the Poor (PDLP), led by Lucio Cabañas until his death in 1974. Both groups were lacking in size and formal structure, and neither had a capacity to seize cities or to gain positions in other states. The Clandestine Workers Revolutionary Party "People's Union" (PROCUP) took shape as an urban wing of the PDLP in the 1970s, though it was also an outgrowth of another armed group, the Unión del Pueblo (People's Union). PROCUP endures to this day, and the fusion between the remnants of the PDLP and PROCUP is such that they are sometimes referred to as PROCUP-PDLP. See Hellman (1988) and Radu (1997).

nalists who have examined the EPR, is quite different. It views the EPR as a network-like alliance among numerous (reportedly 14) armed organizations from all over Mexico (PROCUP included).[7] Some reports also hold that the EPR is the armed front for a broader movement of which the FAC-MLN is the main political front.[8] If the latter story is correct, then the EPR fits better into the netwar framework.

The Zapatista movement has little in common with the darker aspects of Mexico's revolutionary traditions—Chiapas's *indigenas*, the EZLN leadership, and the NGOs are all quite idealistic and have accommodated to the open, democratic ways that can make the network form of organization so appealing. The EPR is a darker phenomenon, so far unameliorated by transnational idealism and reputedly driven by a great bitterness. It emerges in part from one of Mexico's roughest, most feudal states—Guerrero—where violence, crime, and corruption, amplified by drug trafficking, are reigning influences. The EZLN has no known ties to drug traffickers, but the EPR has been suspected of some indirect links.

There is no evidence of direct links between the EZLN and the EPR, and the differences noted above argue against such links. Yet there appear to be indirect links and influences. According to Tello (1995), some guerrillas from PROCUP, one of the constituent elements of the EPR, may have joined the EZLN in its formative days. Also, PROCUP members exploded several bombs around the Mexico City area, damaging at least one electrical power tower, in response to the EZLN's generally futile call in January 1994 for armed uprisings outside Chiapas. But tensions exist between the two groups. And there have been reports that some guerrillas may have left the EZLN for the EPR, because they soured on the EZLN's pacification and wanted to resume the armed struggle.

However, such loose links do not add up to much of a story. The main story may be that the "demonstration effect" of events in Chia-

---

[7]There have also been rumors that the EPR has ties to remnants of European terrorist groups (e.g., ETA and Baader-Meinhof) that have exiles in Mexico.

[8]The EPR has also associated itself with a political party, the Partido Democratico Popular Revolucionario (PDPR), and the two sometimes refer to themselves jointly as the PDPR-EPR .

pas since 1994 catalyzed the EPR's rise, providing evidence that the Zapatista netwar is diffusing—and in more violent directions. This may be the case in either, or both, of two senses. One is that the EPR may aspire to emulate the EZLN's success in gaining concessions from the government (in which case the EPR will eventually agree to negotiate). The other, more documented story is that the EPR may reflect a bitter disappointment in some leftist circles that the EZLN failed to spark nationwide unrest and later relented on the armed struggle. In this story, the FAC-MLN and the EPR are offspring of groups that were critical of, and later expelled by, the EZLN and its leaders at the EZLN-sponsored National Democratic Convention in Chiapas in August 1994. Now, the EPR may be setting out to do what the FLN and the EZLN initially intended but failed to do: mount co-ordinated attacks all over Mexico, drawing on a widely dispersed infrastructure of armed groups operating under a central command or clearinghouse—in other words, a well-coordinated "war of the flea." If so, the EPR is biding its time, since for the past year or so it has refrained from mounting armed attacks, in favor of emphasizing "armed propaganda."

Insofar as combat operations go, the EPR has demonstrated a large view of the battlespace. Apart from showing that it mainly has forces in Guerrero and Oaxaca, it seems to be striking along a central band across Mexico, from the Atlantic to the Pacific coasts. Is it trying to encompass Mexico City? Split the country in half?[9] The EZLN has exhibited little such strategic breadth of vision in the field, confining its military operations to Chiapas while hoping that others around the country would take up arms to follow its example.[10] Indeed, the military postures and requirements of the two organizations are quite different. The EPR has a smaller total force, numbering in the hundreds (perhaps 500–800), but much greater mobility and fire-power. In contrast, the EZLN, which is confined in Chiapas, has come to rely less on military operations and more on maintaining a

---

[9]If so, this would be reminiscent of the Union Anaconda strategy against the Confederacy in the American Civil War, in which it sought to split the South along the Mississippi River.

[10]But if we make a case that the EPR may try to split Mexico from west to east, we should remind ourselves that the EZLN may have intended to spread revolution from south to north, as it was hoping for a northward spillover of revolution from Central America.

small "army in being" whose use may be threatened at critical moments as a way to prod for negotiations.

To say that the EPR is evidence for the diffusion of netwar raises the question as to whether the EPR truly qualifies as (or may develop into) a netwar actor. The evidence for this remains unclear, because so little is known about the EPR. Its pronouncements and actions do not reveal much. It has a general command. But if it has a hierarchical central command presiding over decentralized units, it does not qualify structurally as having a network design, although it may emulate netwar strategies and tactics. If it consists of a set of armed groups and support elements operating as a clandestine all-channel network, with a central clearinghouse for consultation and coordination, then it may be deemed a netwar actor. If so, the EPR represents a different kind of netwar actor from the EZLN. Most likely, the EPR is at least partially networked and aims to wage an armed guerrilla netwar that will emphasize tactically dispersed, nonlinear, swarming operations. As noted, the EPR has already shown a capacity to launch coordinated hit-and-run attacks in various states, in both urban and rural areas.

The EPR has displayed some cleverness at information operations. An example lies in the invitations and bus tickets for journalists to arrive at a particular time and place where, unbeknownst to each other, they expected to conduct interviews with EPR leaders but instead found themselves witnessing an EPR attack on a government building. Moreover, the EPR has insisted, after mounting a number of armed assaults in 1996, that it would focus on "armed propaganda." But so far, notwithstanding the fact that the EPR can gain media coverage with theatrical pronouncements and interviews and has WWW pages in Italy and the Netherlands,[11] information operations do not appear to be its forte.

Despite these contrasts, both the EZLN and the EPR have shown a creativity at modifying traditional notions of guerrilla warfighting. The fact that the EPR has been more violent than the EZLN does not rule out the possibility that the EPR may shift to negotiations at some point. Nor does the mostly pacific tone of EZLN behavior since its

---

[11]At http://www.pengo.it/PDPR-EPR/, and at http://www.xs4all.nl/~insurg.

1994 guarantee that it will continue always to prefer information operations to open fighting. Meanwhile, a remark by military analyst Michael Radu (1997, p. 44) about Chiapas and the EZLN may apply equally well to Guerrero, Oaxaca, and the EPR: "The Mexican government is losing control in the southeast not so much to the militarily weak insurgents as to chaos and anarchy."

THE ZAPATISTA NETWAR GOES GLOBAL

Meanwhile, the EZLN, Marcos in particular, and some activists have endeavored to extend the Zapatista movement by generating a global dimension. The main vehicles for this were the "Intercontinental Encounters." At the first, in July–August 1996 in Chiapas, a working group with participants from around the world lauded the importance of communications for the Zapatista movement and its ability to project its ideas. The group suggested creating an "International Network of Hope," whose design would be "horizontal," "self-organizing," and "without centralized coordination" (all terms that could have been taken from a theory of networks and netwars).

Seeing this as a way to promote a global struggle against neoliberalism, Marcos proposed in his closing address

> that we will make a collective network of all our particular struggles and resistances. An intercontinental network of resistance against neoliberalism . . . in which distinct resistances may support one another. This intercontinental network of resistance is not an organizing structure; it doesn't have a central head or decision maker; it has no central command or hierarchies. We are the network, all of us who resist.

This multiorganizational network will be based on an "intercontinental network of alternative communication," so that all participants can communicate with each other. It "will search to weave the channels so that words may travel all the roads that resist," again in a way that has no hierarchical or centralized design.[12]

---

[12]From text of "Words of the Zapatista Army of National Liberation in the Closing Act of the First Intercontinental Encounter for Humanity and Against Neoliberalism" as read by Subcomandante Insurgente Marcos, at La Realidad, Chiapas, August 3, 1996, published in the *La Jornada*, August 4, 1996, pp. 10–11, translated by the Chiapas

To keep moving down this path as Marcos proposed, the "Second Intercontinental Encounter for Humanity and Against Neoliberalism" was held in Spain in July 1997. The run-up to it, which generated papers posted at Web sites on the Internet, and the gathering itself, which was attended mainly by European activists from Germany, Italy and Spain, took up the challenge of building these global "network(s) for struggle and resistance." Discussions were hampered, however, by the fact that many participants had not attended the "First Intercontinental Encounter" and thus had little background on the idea that the Left should be building networks rather than parties or other traditional organizations. Very few preparatory documents even addressed the notion of networks. More to the point, those participants who were prepared often sounded far from enthusiastic—many voiced views that were cautionary, even doubtful.

In the critical documents,[13] "network" was deemed a very unclear concept. At worst, it was a new "buzzword of the internationalized Left" and might not even be a progressive form of organization (since networks were already a mainstay of corporate and conservative actors). It seemed more a "metaphor" than a "structure" that could be truly developed. And if it could, there were still many questions: Should the emphasis be on social, technological, or organizational networks—and what should be the balance between formal and informal networking? There was agreement to avoid hierarchy, but too much decentralization and informality could mean that things did not get done properly (as in some of the planning for the conference). Questions were also raised as to how best to coordinate global struggles via network designs without requiring some degree of unity, but also without jeopardizing the autonomy and diversity of the members. Furthermore, worries were voiced that activists' inter-

---

Urgent Call for the National Commission for Democracy in Mexico (NCDM), and circulated on the Internet. This text is also known as the "Second Declaration of Reality for Humanity and Against Neoliberalism." For comment, see Peter Brown, "Zapatistas Launch International Network of Hope," dated August 3, 1996 (as circulated on the Internet, August 28, 1996).

[13]The following paragraphs draw mainly on Cleaver (1998), Group 2828 (1997), Wray (1997), an e-mail posting by Harry Cleaver, "Responses to 'Entangled in the Net?'" July 8, 1997, and a few workshop reports that appeared in e-mail postings. It appears from these documents that German participants were the most critical, and Americans the most positive, about the potential of networks for the Left.

ests in addressing local issues could get lost in the quest for global networks. Finally, a root question kept coming up: What is the purpose, the objective—what is it that we really want to do by way of networks?

Because of such issues, the "Second Encounter" ended anticlimactically, leaving considerable uncertainty as to how activists should, and could, best go about building on existing networks and creating new ones. The aim should be, as an American noted, "to weave a variety of struggles into one struggle that never loses its multiplicity" (Cleaver, 1998). But, perhaps partly because the Zapatista movement was so much the *cause celebre* of the gathering, the skeptics and critics evidently needed reminding that a worldwide trend in favor of networked social movements was already well under way in Europe and North America:

> [T]he groundwork for the Zapatista use of the Net was laid by the continent-wide organizing against the North American Free Trade Agreement. PeaceNet and its plethora of conferences, mobilization against the Gulf War via the Net, the European Counter Network, etc. all predated the Zapatista uprising. It has been a spectacularly successful example of the potential of computer communications for the rapid international circulation of struggle to the point of becoming emblematic, but it is only one among many. The problem the encounter must address is what kind of connections can be established among the diversity of existing "networks" and other forms of organization that can facilitate and accelerate resistance and struggle in such a way as to intensify the disruption and destructuring of the various mechanisms and structures of capitalist power and open new spaces and create new capabilities for crafting alternatives.[14]

Thus, Marcos, the EZLN, and the Zapatista movement sought to achieve a global reach. They wanted the conflict in Chiapas to represent an opening salvo in what they believed should be not only a national but also a global struggle against the defects of neoliberalism, capitalism, and the market system. A global reaction to neoliberalism may well emerge (see Fuller, 1995). And it may be sensible

---

[14]From the e-mail posting by Harry Cleaver, "Responses to 'Entangled in the Net?'" July 8, 1997.

for Marcos and the EZLN to gamble in this direction, whether or not it has a large effect on what happens to them in Mexico. But the "Second Intercontinental Encounter" did not yield any particular near-term tactical or strategic advantages for them. At the moment, no plans are unfolding for a third international gathering.

ASSESSMENTS OF THE EZLN/ZAPATISTA MOVEMENT

What are analysts to make of the significance of the Zapatista phenomenon? A concluding passage in Carlos Tello's 1995 study of the EZLN sums up well the range of effects, most of them double-edged and contradictory, that many analysts, Mexican and otherwise, continue to attribute to the conflict in Chiapas:

> The uprising shook the nation's conscience; put an end to the government's triumphalism; reraised the indigenous question; put the problem of marginalization and poverty . . . at the top of the country's priorities; and also added, along with other factors, to the pressures for a democratic transition. At the same time, however, it divided [peoples'] consciences; destabilized markets; increased [the level of] violence; and sowed a lack of trust by Mexicans in their institutions. In the conflict zone, as in the rest of the country, the rebellion's consequences were also contradictory. The uprising reactivated the flow of resources to the communities; accelerated the resolution of the peasants' land problems; revolutionized the norms for imparting justice; and impelled changes that the electoral law required in Chiapas. At the same time, however, it caused dozens of deaths in a few days; broke up families; provoked the expulsion of thousands of *indigenas* from their villages; left many poor ranchers without a means of subsistence; increased [the level of] insecurity in the countryside; and led to the militarization of the *Cañadas.* (Tello, 1995, p. 209, translation.)

Partly because there are so many ambiguities and contradictions, not to mention uncertainties, stemming from the fact that conflict continues, most analysts—particularly in Mexico and particularly on the Left—remain divided in their overall assessments of the EZLN and the broader Zapatista movement. An argument can be made, as in the following statement by Carlos Fuentes, a leading Mexican intellectual, that the Zapatista movement has had a profoundly positive

effect because it compounded the pressures on the Mexican government to pursue political and other reforms:

> You must never forget that the Mexican political process owes a
> great deal to Subcomandante Marcos and the Zapatistas. Without
> the political earthquake of January 1994—which demonstrated that
> unless quick progress was made to solve the country's political
> problems there would be outbursts of insurgency—it would have
> been impossible to begin a new political era. That was the warning
> from Subcomandante Marcos, and President Carlos Salinas de
> Gortari understood it. Thanks to the Chiapas insurrection and the
> political response of Salinas, that new era has begun.[15]

But a contrary view, represented here in the words of Jorge
Castañeda, another leading intellectual, has turned to depreciating
the Zapatista movement:

> The 1,111 Zapatista activists or sympathizers marching on Mexico
> City last week [September 1996] were a painful and sad symbol of
> the predicament their movement has gotten itself into. Having cap-
> tured the imagination of the media and solidarity groups the world
> over, and having achieved real support within the rank and file of
> Mexican public opinion and the left, Subcommander Marcos and
> his well-organized indigenous communities have reached a dead
> end. Or rather, the dead end they plunged into a couple of years
> ago has become woefully apparent.[16]

These two stances pretty much bound the spectrum of analysis, indi-
cating that years of debate lie ahead about the effects and implications of this seminal case.

Analyzing Causality and Credit—A Difficult Task

Our interviews for this study suggest that a cautioning word is in order regarding assertions as to who has caused what, and who de-

---

[15]From an interview with Carlos Fuentes, by Alejandro Escalona, "Carlos Fuentes:
Novelist, Social Critic," *The Chicago Tribune,* Sunday, August 3, 1997, as found posted
to Chiapas95 list, August 4, 1997.

[16]Jorge G. Castañeda, "Chiapas 'War' Ends in a Whimper," *Los Angeles Times,*
September 15, 1996. Yet Castañeda initially believed (1994, p. 34) that "This is not a
millenarian Jacquerie; this is a highly current and contemporary guerrilla group."

serves credit for what, in this netwar. Activists have made numerous assertions that particular episodes of activism caused a change in government policy or behavior, and that the NGOs deserve credit for this. Indeed, many activists have eagerly claimed credit for pressuring the government to halt military operations, conduct negotiations, make concessions, and adopt reforms. While some journalists would claim that the media deserves the lion's share of credit for impelling President Salinas or Zedillo to make one policy change or another (e.g., as in calling a cease-fire), many activists would argue that the NGOs deserve more credit than the media for influencing this conflict—and indeed, it was often the activists whom the journalists were interviewing.

Claims of causality and credit emanating from NGOs, and counterclaims from the government, are an important aspect of social netwar (as they are in other modes of conflict). But such claims are a tenuous area for verification and analysis.

For example, it may appear that networked NGOs obliged officials to make some change, but in fact the change (e.g., establishment of a commission, or a halt to military operations) surely had multiple causes. Or what initially appeared to be a change may not prove much of one later (e.g., the government halts a military operation, but then renews it in a slow-motion manner that does not arouse the media or the NGOs). Thus, a "perception management" game may be played, in which the Zapatistas appear to have influence when the government announces concessions or reversals—but then the government quietly returns to business as usual.

In the final analysis, much may depend on the government's willingness to move in the direction of negotiations and concessions. The analyst should thus be wary of easy notions that social movements are the key factor affecting a government's decisions to adopt reforms. They may be an important factor, but as Diane Davis (1994, p. 38) notes in a study of Mexico City during 1982–1988, "the willingness and capacity of governing officials to cede to popular mobilizations, and to introduce certain institutional reforms, may influence the overall extent of democratization as much as the presence of social movements themselves." A similar point may well apply to some aspects of the Chiapas conflict.

Also, claiming credit may cut both ways. On the one hand, the EZLN and some NGOs may claim credit for something in order to argue that their strategies and tactics are working. But on the other hand, at times it may be the government's intention to have the Zapatistas take some credit, to help keep them on a peaceful track and thereby try to institutionalize their behavior.

While many activists argue that the Zapatista movement has had myriad positive effects, some critics and cynics among them doubt the long-range significance. They question whether a new strategy of radical change is really in the making, since they are not convinced that the Zapatistas, their NGO allies, and the use of the new information technologies have really won much, or that Mexico's authoritarian state has really changed much, or that the army has really backed off, or that the U.S. government has become any less influential in Mexico, or that the NGOs have succeeded in getting the U.S. government to pressure Mexico to back away from repression.

The difficulty of determining causation extends to changes in army organization and behavior. Did those changes occur because of Chiapas? Or were many of them on track to occur anyway, because of antinarcotics, counterinsurgency, and institutional concerns—and Chiapas spurred the timing? After all, many of the army's innovations were proposed in documents in the early 1980s but shelved due to a lack of revenues.

In short, the conflict in Chiapas seems to be partly a catalyst and partly a cause of the various changes identified with it. Either way, it has had significant effects, though the debates about the hows and whys of those effects have probably barely begun. A detailed analysis would require more research than this limited study can provide.

Structural Reform and Stability in Mexico

Having noted this, our own work implies the following conclusions: The EZLN is the most significant armed movement in Mexico since the 1970s, and the Zapatista movement writ large is the most significant social movement since the student-led social movement of 1968. What has made the EZLN/Zapatista movement so significant is, in particular, its capacity for nonviolent information operations, spread through all manner of media. These information operations have shaken the Mexican system to its foundations—but they have prompted reform and restructuring more than they have jeopardized Mexico's stability.

The shift from a combat- to an information-oriented netwar enabled the EZLN to acquire legitimacy in the eyes of the Mexican government and the public, and especially global civil society. At the national level, the Zapatistas' netwar strategy succeeded in muddling the government's efforts to crush the insurgency, contrary to the fate of most previous armed rebellions against state authority in Mexico. The centralized state had difficulty dealing with this nonstate movement largely because of its transnational, internetted organization. Even tacit American support for a government crackdown on the EZLN in 1994 did not blunt the NGOs' effectiveness.

The netwar contributed to acute perceptions of crisis and instability, especially in 1994. But this did not have all the effects the Zapatista movement may have intended. The adverse perceptions alarmed foreign investors and creditors, and they contributed to the peso devaluation late that year—thereby weakening the state. Yet earlier in 1994, when many activists shifted their focus from the conflict in Chiapas to aspire to bring about the downfall of the PRI in the national elections, the perceptions of potential crisis and instability stemming from Chiapas led many citizens to vote overwhelmingly for the PRI's candidates—thereby strengthening the state.

Meanwhile, the netwar reignited public debates about Mexico's national identity and economic strategy—debates that had died down after Mexico's acceptance of NAFTA. The Zapatista movement obliged Mexico's rulers to rethink what economic reform should mean in the Mexican context; under President Zedillo, they have pulled back from the headlong neoliberalism that prevailed under President Salinas. This might have happened anyway—for example, there is no clear link between the Chiapas conflict and the October 1996 decision to halt the full privatization of the petrochemical industry—but the Zapatista movement contributed to a reshaping of the information environment on this score.

Overall, the netwar has helped impel the Mexican government to continue down the road of reform. It added to the pressures on Mexico's leaders to enact political and electoral reforms; to make the political party system more transparent, accountable, and democratic; to take human rights more seriously; to accept the rise of civil society; and to heed anew the needs of indigenous peoples. Some analysts claim that political and electoral reform has proceeded faster since the Zapatista movement than in years past.

Curiously, the Zapatista netwar, though leftist in nature, has neither benefited, nor benefited from, what traditional leftists view as the most "legitimate" force for political and electoral change in Mexico: the Democratic Revolutionary Party (PRD). The PRD suffered nationally, along with other parties, from the activities of the Zapatistas, whose leaders, notably Marcos, refused to identify the EZLN with support for any political party and called instead for civil society to assume the leading role in bringing about social change in Mexico.

NGO activism has its limitations, but this case shows that nonstate actors have growing abilities to constrain state actors. Both the transnational and Mexican NGOs altered the dynamics of the confrontation in Chiapas, converting a primarily military situation into a political one. Their involvement assured, in conjunction with the media, that what might once have been kept a local problem became, and remained, a national and international event. They altered the context for decisionmaking in Mexico City and, in so doing, impelled the government to agree to negotiations with the EZLN, kept the military at bay, and constrained the government from irrevocably painting the EZLN as a body of "terrorists" and "criminals."

The continued potential for violence in Chiapas, and the diffusion of insurgency (not to mention criminality, and possibly terrorism) to other parts of Mexico, make the Mexican political system appear unbalanced. It often seems to be under attack on multiple fronts by a variety of netwar adversaries—and neither the fronts nor the adversaries are always clearly discernible. Despite this, it is not certain that Mexico's overall political stability is at risk. It certainly isn't from the EZLN.

Government and army resources, though strained, seem adequate to cope with the current array of adversaries. Whether Mexico can continue to cope with them and preserve its stability is an important question that gets repeatedly asked in Mexico, the United States, and elsewhere. One answer, according to our understanding of networks and netwars, is strategic: Mexico's prospects for stability and for success in dealing with multiple netwars—the social netwar identified with the EZLN, the armed netwar pursued by the EPR, and the criminal netwar represented by the internetted drug cartels—will depend on the government's ability to form its own inter-organizational and multiagency networks to confront and counter those netwars. By understanding the nature of netwar, and by examining Mexico's successes in dealing with the EZLN, the Mexican government and military may derive general principles that will help guide them to solutions for dealing with the EPR and other armed radical groups, and with the cartels.

Indeed, the serious potential future risk for Mexico is not an old-fashioned civil war or another social revolution—those kinds of scenarios are unlikely. The greater risk is a plethora of social, guerrilla, and criminal netwars. Mexico's security (or insecurity) in the information age may be increasingly a function of netwars of all varieties. Mexico is already the scene of more types of divisive, stressful netwars than other societies at a similar level of development, in part because it is a neighbor of the United States.

At present, neither social (EZLN/Zapatista), guerrilla (EPR), or criminal (drug trafficking) netwar actors seem likely to make Mexico ungovernable or to create a situation that leads to a newly authoritarian regime. This *might* occur, if these netwars all got interlaced and reinforced each other, directly or indirectly, in conditions where an economic recession deepens, the federal government and the PRI (presumably still in power) lose legitimacy to an alarming degree, and infighting puts the elite "revolutionary family" and its political clans into chaos. But all this seems quite unlikely, since, owing to the deepening of structural reforms, Mexico may be in better shape now than in the early and middle 1980s, when some analysts (e.g., Castañeda, 1986; Latell, 1986) argued that breakdown or collapse was probably imminent. However, an eye should be kept on the period just before, during, and after the year 2000 elections. Will this provide a propitious time for an old-guard *Priista* with criminal bearings to gain his party's presidential nomination? For armed groups like the EPR to take to the field? For a subtle interplay to develop between gangster and guerrilla groups that leads to the imposition of a heavy-handed regime whose darker purposes might include strategic crime and criminal mercantilism?[17]

Mexico faces a continuing challenge of coping with all manner of netwars, not to mention other kinds of disturbances, in ways that assure both the continued stability and reformability of the Mexican system. Both dynamics, stability and reformability, are at stake; and there is no easy relationship between them—sometimes stability is enhanced by economic and political reforms, other times it can be disturbed by them. If Mexico does not develop a sound capacity for counternetwar, there is a risk that the country, even though it remains stable, could succumb to a criminalization scenario or see its capacity for reform and transformation become so confounded that a "stuck system" scenario prevails.[18]

Winners and Losers?

Against this background of the netwar's uneven effects on Mexico's stability and reform processes, it remains far from clear whether the EZLN and the government are headed more toward a "win-win," a "lose-lose," or a mixed outcome. At first, when it looked as though the EZLN's insurrection would lead to a classic insurgency-counterinsurgency, the likely outcome was bound to be "win-lose." Both the government and the EZLN could not win when the EZLN was proclaiming violent revolution. But, partly because of the moderating effects that the NGOs had on both sides' initial tendencies to seek a violent solution, a "win-win" solution has seemed a possibility at times. During 1996, for example, the government said it sought "a dignified peace with neither winners or losers." Indeed, social netwar, by being less destructive than armed insurgency, makes room for compromise peace agreements.

Why has a "win-win" solution seemed possible? Neither side has pursued the total demise of the other. Each side has shown at least a modicum of respect for the other. Negotiations have led to concessions, notably by the government on respect for indigenous rights

---

[17]We are indebted to round-table musings at an academic conference in Washington, D.C. for surfacing some of these dark speculations.

[18]See Appendix B for an experimental explanation and analysis.

and cultural autonomy (although the government is now going slow on implementation). In the process, the EZLN has gone from looking like a real or potential threat to something more like a protracted challenge. The possibility remains that it will convert from a military into a political force—although one of its created agencies for doing so, the Zapatista National Liberation Front (FZLN), is not showing much promise. Meanwhile, another consideration that has augured for a "win-win" outcome is that, as noted above, the political, electoral, and other reform processes have been reinforced during this period.

That all sides have kept their behavior in a nationalist framework is another important factor that has kept this conflict on a "win-win" track. Mexicans take their nationalism very, very seriously. The EZLN was quick to deny that it was foreign in origin and repeatedly averred it was a Mexican movement. More to the point, it has resisted allying with movements that are not nationalist. Some NGO activists, notably in the area of indigenous rights, wanted the EZLN to express its solidarity with their transnational agenda, but Marcos and other leaders declined to do so. The EZLN has also not posed as a cross-border Mayan irredentist movement. Had the EZLN cast aside its Mexican nationalist credentials, the government and the army might have had a solid pretext, and public support, for quashing it.

For a "win-win" outcome to become likely, Mexico's civilian and military leaders have to use the army adroitly. By now, it seems clear that the EZLN's putative power and influence depends on its political support from the activist world, that it poses a symbolic more than a real threat of violence, and that its military capabilities are minor. Since 1995, the army has slowly but surely reasserted a dominant presence in the conflict zone. It has gained the upper hand militarily, showing that the EZLN is a weak "paper tiger" (though it has proved itself a "cyber tiger"). A well-behaved presence in and around the conflict zone would help keep pressure on the EZLN's leaders to seek a negotiated outcome; it would also help keep the activist NGOs involved, even though that results mostly in criticism of the army's presence and the behavior of its soldiers in the zone.

But these will be moot points, and the likelihood of a "win-win" outcome may deteriorate sharply (as it did during much of 1997) if armed netwar and/or traditional insurgency diffuse throughout the country. Indeed, the attractiveness of netwar as a method of disruption for other dissidents and rebels raises the possibility of emulation and diffusion throughout Mexico, which, should it occur extensively, would surely imperil the peace and strain the government and army to their limits. If this occurs, and the rise of the EPR indicates it may, the possibility of a combative "lose-lose" outcome could increase significantly.

ACTORS TO WATCH: THE MILITARY AND THE NGOs

Which scenarios materialize in Mexico may well depend on large-scale political, economic, social, and other forces. But it is also the case that when a society has become disorderly and out of equilibrium as a result of a systemic transition, actors that might normally be marginal may have decisive effects.[19] This study of the Zapatista netwar suggests that the Mexican military and the NGOs may be two such actors.

The Chiapas experience indicates that the Mexican military is capable of doctrinal and organizational innovation. A range of positive changes (a move to smaller units, to decentralized tactical control, etc.) should serve as force multipliers and modifiers for the 130,000-man Mexican army, allowing it to wage counternetwar on multiple fronts. Indeed, it may be advisable for the army to avoid falling back on its traditional reliance on firepower and mass movement as it seeks to engage the EPR or other armed groups. In the new conflict zones in Guerrero and Oaxaca, it would also seem advisable for the army to avoid falling back on its old heavy-handed methods of counterinsurgency, which end up alienating more local people than they intimidate. Ironically, U.S. military assurances of the availability of material support for counterinsurgency may discourage the Mexican army from pursuing innovative operations against the EPR. Indeed, there may be a lesson here for U.S. military assistance—that, in cases like this, "less is more."

---

[19]This proposition comes from recent studies about "chaos" and "complex adaptive systems." A good introduction is Waldrop (1992).

Another lesson of the Zapatista experience for counternetwar is that local and transnational civil-society NGOs have risen in influence and cannot be disregarded. Since they continue to constrain the government's military responses to the EZLN and to be stern and unrelenting critics of the Mexican political system, it is only natural that the government should regard them as problems, if not adversaries. But perhaps the government should increasingly find ways to reach out to the NGOs as an asset.[20] They have helped keep the EZLN in line during a difficult period—they have periodically helped in restarting the stalled negotiations in Chiapas, and they have made the conflict one of ideas rather than shootings. A government-NGO embrace seems out of the question—each is bound to keep its distance from the other. But better bridge-building may be advisable. It is not just coping with the EZLN that is at stake; government and NGO actors have mutual interests in seeing condemnations of the violent, destructive acts of the EPR and of the drug cartels' depredations. This might go a long way toward helping calm the fears of investors in Mexico and elsewhere.

In other words, the Mexican military and the NGOs are the bracketing forces in this conflict. Moreover, they are among the most counterpoised actors on the Mexican scene; many among them even regard each other as enemies. The military is part of Mexico's statist hierarchies; it is steeped in the traditions of closed nationalism and is responsible for preserving constitutional order. In contrast, the NGOs are part of the emerging antihierarchical, multiorganizational networks of the information age; many are amenable to transnational ties and eager to pressure for reform. The backgrounds, cultures, interests, and ideological orientations found among military officers and NGO activists are generally at odds. In Chiapas they are committed to supporting opposing sides in the conflict; they have a very uneasy relationship in all other matters.

The military and the NGOs are bound to keep eyeing each other with suspicion and distrust. Yet the balance between stability and instability, between advance and regression, could be tipped by the roles that each plays. Mexico's prospects for stability and reform might be

---

[20]By which we mean information-age civil-society NGOs, not the uncivil-society NGOs that the government traditionally reaches out to in times of insecurity: local paramilitary forces and *cacique*-led organizations.

enhanced if the sides could learn to understand each other and work together better in at least some limited issue areas (e.g., human-rights monitoring or electoral monitoring). Expecting them to become allies or partners in the pursuit of conflict resolution would be expecting too much. In some senses, however, they need each other—but they do not know it, and probably do not want to know it.

Dealing with civil-society NGOs—whether as allies, as in some humanitarian and disaster relief operations, or as antagonists, as in some instances of human-rights and environmental abuse—is a new frontier for government officials and military officers around the world. In the period ahead in Mexico, the government and the military may at times be tempted to repress some local NGOs and restrict freedom of information, in the name of security. But that could ignore the important, positive roles that NGOs are generally likely to play in the information age. Without a diverse transnational presence, presumably of responsible NGOs (and corporations), Mexico would probably not make a strong effort to evolve into an open, democratic system that can benefit all sectors of society.[21]

Yet there is a conundrum. Neither the military, which is statist in orientation, nor the NGOs, which contain many leftists and center-leftists, seem to favor Mexico's full transition to an open market economy. It is not clear that either actor has much belief that the construction of an economically advanced, politically democratic system requires a market system. If statist preferences continue to prevail within both actors, their increased activism may unwittingly help keep much of Mexico locked in its traditional preferences for corporatist approaches to its development.

Of course, this is not inevitable; their activism will be balanced by that of other actors in Mexico. Moreover, the previous point may be too generalized; a cross-sectional analysis of the military and the NGOs may well show that significant sectors of them do believe that the market system can be beneficial for Mexico, so long as it is prop-

---

[21]In like manner, Sergio Aguayo, "Mexico Must Get Used to Foreign Scrutiny," *Los Angeles Times*, April 26, 1998, p. M5, observes that: "Our challenge now is to reconcile our nationalism, with all its historic suspicions toward foreigners, with an ever more interdependent relationship with our international partners. If our doors are open to foreign business, they must also be open to the human rights community."

erly elaborated. In that case, these actors will not constrain Mexico's transition and may help strengthen and guide it. Indeed, some NGO networks, notably groupings like the Civic Alliance, have pressured the electoral and party systems to adopt reforms and become more open and competitive.

Meanwhile, since a social netwar is not a traditional insurgency, part of the challenge in Mexico is to recognize (as has partially occurred) that military, security, and police roles rarely figure large in counternetwar involving social actors. The army learned in 1994 that it was not accustomed to dealing with civil-society actors clamoring for access and information in Chiapas, and it has been making some adjustments to improve its behavior toward NGOs.

All this may have implications for Mexico's national security concept. Indeed, the advent of social netwar, in the context of Mexico's broader structural transformation, may induce a rethinking of aspects of Mexico's concept. For at least a decade, national security has been defined in "integral" terms—the concept has emphasized a combination of political, social, economic, and military dimensions, with the military accepting, if not insisting, that the military dimensions be subordinate to the civilian. In 1980, then Secretary of National Defense General Felix Galván Lopez gave the concept its tone when he remarked, "I understand by national security the maintenance of social, economic, and political *equilibrium*, guaranteed by the armed forces."[22] The Zapatista netwar has called attention to the fact that Mexico is adapting, with difficulty, to political and electoral reforms, the growth of a market system, the rise of civil society, and shifting balances of power and priorities in terms of federal, state, and local relations. If Mexico can continue to adapt successfully, it will mean a new "equilibrium," and this will surely prompt a reevaluation of what is meant by "national security."

---

[22]From an article in the magazine *Proceso,* September 22, 1980, p. 6 (translation; italics added).

BASIC IMPLICATION FOR U.S. MILITARY POLICY: "GUARDED OPENNESS"

Ultimately, netwar and counternetwar become a game not only of power but also of vision, responsibility, and adaptability. Is Mexico up to this challenge? Mexico's state retains substantial power relative to its mix of adversaries. But the cumulative pressures of having to cope with several different types of netwar on several fronts is likely to keep the government and the military on edge, alternating between, on the one hand, the pursuit of forward-looking policies and strategies that are attuned to a new vision of inclusive democratic governance, and on the other hand, an episodic reversion to traditional policies and strategies that reflect a time, not more than a decade or two ago, when a heavy-handed mix of military and paramilitary measures was a preferred way to safeguard public order, especially in provincial areas.

Because the EZLN, the EPR, and other armed groups seem quite unlikely to be able to cause major political instability, U.S. analysts would be well advised to adopt a tempered rather than alarmist view of Mexico.[23] Even if U.S. analysts see fit to appraise the potential for instability there, they should not truly expect it to occur. There is little reason for U.S. relations with the Mexican military to be driven by insurgency scenarios. Gangsters pose more of a threat than guerrillas do to Mexico's future and U.S. interests.

Since the middle 1990s, both the U.S. and Mexican militaries have had new, though distinct, incentives for seeking closer cooperation; and cooperation has been growing. The U.S. military should be attentive to the Mexican military's requests and initiatives for neighborly advice and assistance—if only to surmount the fact that it has as many disappointments about past U.S. behavior as the U.S. military has about past Mexican unresponsiveness to various U.S. initiatives. But because the Mexican military seems likely to revert at times to heavy-handed policies and strategies, it is advisable for the U.S. military to be wary of very close association.

An appropriate principle for neighborly U.S. military relations with the Mexican military may well be "guarded openness," a deliberately

---

[23]See Appendix B for a discussion.

ambivalent concept from the new field of information strategy that means being forthcoming about providing and sharing information in areas of mutual benefit where trust and confidence are high, yet being self-protective in areas where trust and confidence are not adequate (see Arquilla and Ronfeldt, 1997).[24] From the perspective of guarded openness, what may be needed most in the case of U.S.-Mexico military relations is the construction of a "culture of cooperation"—indeed, a binational "military noosphere" (see Arquilla and Ronfeldt, forthcoming)—in which the emphasis will be on what ideas and values can be shared and elaborated conjointly, rather than on what U.S. equipment and techniques can be provided.

_____

[24]For additional, broader, and more specific commentary on the options for U.S.-Mexican military relations, see Bailey and Aguayo (1996) and Schulz (1995).

Chapter Seven

BEYOND MEXICO

As noted in Chapter One, the Zapatista case has been hailed from the beginning as the world's first "postmodern" insurgency or movement. As such, it has generated enormous comment outside as well as inside Mexico, and much of that has involved whether, and how, this case offers an information-age model of social struggle that can be further developed and replicated elsewhere.

That view is not without critics. For example, writing from a rather traditional leftist position, Daniel Nugent (1995) has decried the postmodern label by pointing out that the EZLN remains quite traditional and premodern in many respects:

> It is difficult to see how a rebel army of peasants, aware of itself as the product of five hundred years of struggle, that quotes from the Mexican constitution to legitimate its demand that the president of Mexico immediately leave office, that additionally demands work, land, housing, food, health, education, independence, liberty, democracy, justice, and peace for the people of Mexico, can be called a "postmodern political movement." How can the EZLN move beyond the politics of modernity when their vocabulary is so patently modernist and their practical organization so emphatically pre-modern? Their democratic command structure is a slow-moving form of organization—requiring as it does direct consultation and discussion with the base communities in five or six different languages—which is difficult to reconcile with postmodernist digital simultaneity. Do their demands include a modem and VCR in every jacale or adobe hut in Mexico? No. Is their chosen name "The Postmodern Army of Multinational Emancipation" or "Cyber-warriors of the South"? No.

But his points draw sharp dividing lines between what is deemed premodern, modern, or postmodern. The marvel, according to Chris Hables Gray (1997, pp. 5–6), in opening his book *Postmodern War,* is that the Zapatistas represent a hybrid of all three eras, and in a sense to be a hybrid is to be postmodern:

> Theirs is a hybrid movement, with the traditional virtues of peasant rebellions augmented by media-savvy spokespeople who use the internet and the tabloid press with the shamelessness of athletic shoe companies. . . . [Marcos] is clearly part of a sophisticated attempt by the Zapatistas to break their political isolation with a strange combination of small unit attacks, national mobilizations, and international appeals. . . . Victory, for Marcos, isn't achieving state power, it is reconfiguring power.

Irrespective of whether the postmodern label is applied, there is no denying that information plays a seminal, decisive role in this movement. As Manuel Castells (1997, p. 79) points out, in an important, wide-ranging discussion about how the information age may affect the nature of social conflict around the world,

> The success of the *Zapatistas* was largely due to their communication strategy, to the point that they can be called the *first informational guerrilla movement.* They created a media event in order to diffuse their message, while desperately trying not to be brought into a bloody war. . . . The *Zapatistas'* ability to communicate with the world, and with Mexican society, propelled a local, weak insurgent group to the forefront of world politics.

And his points are not unique to the Zapatistas. As a result of the information revolution, a range of new social movements—Castells also discusses environmental, religious fundamentalist, women's liberation, and American militia movements—are being redefined by the rise of a "networking, decentered form of organization and intervention" (p. 362). What is important about these networks is not just their ability to organize activities, but also to produce their own "cultural codes" and then disseminate them throughout societies:

> Because our historical vision has become so used to orderly battalions, colorful banners, and scripted proclamations of social change, we are at a loss when confronted with the subtle pervasiveness of incremental changes of symbols processed through multi-

form networks, away from the halls of power. (Castells, 1997, p. 362.)

The Mexican case is so seminal that Harry Cleaver (1997) speaks of a "Zapatista effect" that may spread contagiously to other societies:

> Beyond plunging the political system into crisis in Mexico, the Zapatista struggle has inspired and stimulated a wide variety of grassroots political efforts in many other countries. . . . it is perhaps not exaggerated to speak of a "Zapatista Effect" reverberating through social movements around the world—homologous to, but ultimately much more threatening to the New World Order of neo-liberalism than the "Tequila Effect" that rippled through emerging financial markets in the wake of the Peso Crisis of 1994.

Anti-Maastricht marches in Europe, and the roles played by Zapatista-inspired Italian radicals, are among the examples he cites. But his analytical point is broader than any single example: a new "electronic fabric of struggle" is being constructed, helping to interconnect and inspire activist movements around the world (Cleaver, 1995c, 1998).[1]

We should note that there is some intellectual circularity in our presentation here. Most of the writings that we cite and quote from as evidence for the rise of netwar are by authors (e.g., Castells, Cleaver, Hables) who cite and quote from our original work proposing the netwar concept (especially Arquilla and Ronfeldt, 1993, 1996b). However, this circularity does not invalidate our using their writings as evidence for the spread of netwar. Instead, it confirms, as have discussions at the two Intercontinental Encounters organized by the

---

[1]As the final touches were being put on this study, further evidence for this point appeared with news reports that a coalition of transnational civil-society NGOs, including the Council of Canadians and the Malaysia-based Third World Network, making use of the Internet and other media, had "routed" international negotiations that were supposed to lead to a Multilateral Agreement on Investment (MAI). "The success of that networking was clear this week when ministers from the 29 countries in the Organization for Economic Cooperation and Development admitted that the global wave of protest had swamped the deal." Some of the Canadians involved in this network had previously been active in anti-NAFTA networking. See Madelaine Drohan, "How the Net Killed the MAI: Grassroots Groups Used Their Own Globalization to Derail Deal," *The Globe and Mail*, April 29, 1998—as posted on the Internet.

Zapatistas, that the "network" meme[2] is taking hold in intellectual and activist circles and diffusing to new places around the world.

Thus, Chiapas provides the first of what may become a plethora of social netwars in the years ahead. Each may have its own characteristics, depending on the country and region in which it occurs. Chiapas, partly because it is an early case, may turn out to be a special case; so we should beware of generalizing from it. Yet it is portentous. To the extent that we can generalize from it, some lessons and implications appear to be as follows.

TOWARD A DEMOGRAPHY OF SOCIAL NETWAR

The Mexican case shows that social netwar is an organizational and technological phenomenon; it depends on the growing presence both of activist NGOs and of all manner of information and communications technologies. As both presences grow around the world—and they are likely to continue growing—the incidence of social netwar is likely to grow. There may well be a synergistic relationship between the rise of the NGOs and the new technologies. As one activist we interviewed stated, "The Net is only useful to the extent that it is able to feed an activist mechanism." Accordingly, the Internet may create a synergy between the producers and the receivers of information, enabling different groups to make contacts and find new allies.

The numbers of NGOs has exploded in the past two decades, and even though many are having funding and other problems, the numbers are likely to keep growing throughout the world. Providing a demographic survey of the data on this lies beyond the limitations of this project. But, to quote from Adrienne Goss (1995), it appears that a global "third sector" is being created—"a massive array of self-governing private organizations, not dedicated to distributing profits

---

[2]Dawkins (1989) originated the notion of memes as a postgenetic basis for continued human evolution, in order to convey his point that cultural as well as biological bodies are based on units of "self-replicating patterns of information" (p. 329). In his view (p. 192), "Just as genes propagate themselves in the gene pool by leaping from body to body via sperm or eggs, so memes propagate themselves in the meme pool by leaping from brain to brain via a process which, in the broad sense, can be called imitation." Lynch (1996) discusses how memes spread through "thought contagion."

to shareholders or directors, pursuing public purposes outside the formal apparatus of the state."[3] This amounts to an "associational revolution" among nonstate actors that may prove as significant as the rise of the nation state.[4]

Most NGOs are hungry for the new information technologies, since they realize that communications is one of their key challenges and assets. Some NGOs in fact specialize in transferring the technologies to other NGOs, in order to ensure that their networks expand and become better and easier to use. Of these, the most important remains the Association for Progressive Communications (APC), which, as discussed earlier, is a worldwide partnership of member networks (like Peacenet and Conflictnet) that provides low-cost computer-communication services and information-sharing tools to individuals and NGOs working on social issues. In 1995, the APC had over fifty member networks in sixteen countries, and it provided access to 20,000 activists in 133 countries in fifteen languages (Goss, 1995)— and the numbers have risen since then.

Although netwar does not necessarily require access to the latest generation of information and communication technologies and does not depend specifically on the Internet, clearly some such communications infrastructure is necessary for NGOs to communicate with each other and to get their messages out to broad audiences. While the technologies need not be widely available, they should be sufficiently widespread that NGOs with limited budgets and resources can make consistent use of them. This point reflects our argument that strong local NGOs are essential for the transnational NGOs to network with.[5]

Again, the numbers are going up with respect to peoples' access to all manner of the new technologies. Nonetheless, it is well known that

---

[3]Goss (1995) is selected for quotation because her article was circulated on Chiapas-related lists on the Internet. For a separate, extensive discussion of the notion of a "third sector," see Rifkin (1995).

[4]Ronfeldt (1996) speaks to these points and offers an extensive bibliography. Recent policy-oriented additions to the literature include Mathews (1997) and Slaughter (1997).

[5]Imagine if the EZLN and local groups had refused to embrace the transnational NGOs and had denounced them as imperialists instead of describing their efforts as vital for peace and reform.

good access to the Internet is available in only a relatively small number of countries, and mostly only among the wealthier, more educated people. Americans are the heaviest users of the Internet, Europeans the second heaviest. In the Third World, Internet access is still spotty, and not particularly good where it does exist—and that applies to large parts of Mexico. In general, the "have-nots" still vastly outnumber the "haves."[6] However, Internet connectivity and bandwidth are expanding rapidly around the world. Even relatively "closed" countries like Cuba and Iran have Internet connections now.

Meanwhile, the world is moving rapidly beyond the era of faxes and text-only e-mail. Before long, activists will be able to upload full-motion audio-video files from inexpensive, handheld cameras. Moreover, in the next decade, satellite telephony may become a widespread reality. Activists will be able to upload and download materials from even remote locations, without having to go through a telephone system that may be controlled by a local government. Governments may have no way to prevent this sort of transmission. In short, radical improvements lie ahead for the NGOs' abilities to communicate and share information, and these improvements may become widely available as costs come down.

EVOLUTION OF ORGANIZATION, DOCTRINE, AND STRATEGY

The Mexican case instructs that militant NGO-based activism is the cutting edge of social netwar, especially where it assumes trans-national dimensions. A transnational network structure is taking shape, in which both issue-oriented and infrastructure-building NGOs are important for the development of social netwar. This infrastructure is growing, so that the activism it enables can extend from the locale where issues are generated (e.g., Chiapas) to the distant hallways of policymakers and decisionmakers (including in Washington, D.C.).

------

[6]Goss (1995), Kedzie (1995), and Swett (1995), not to mention other sources, give extensive statistical details.

The case instructs that netwar depends on the emergence of "swarm networks,"[7] and that swarming best occurs where dispersed NGOs are internetted and collaborate in ways that exhibit "collective diversity" and "coordinated anarchy." The paradoxical tenor of these phrases is intentional. The swarm engages NGOs that have diverse, specialized interests; thus, any issue can be rapidly singled out and attacked by at least elements of the swarm. At the same time, many NGOs can act, and can see themselves acting, as part of a collectivity in which they share convergent ideological and political ideals and similar concepts about nonviolent strategy and tactics. While some NGOs may be more active and influential than others, the collectivity has no central leadership or command structure; it is multiheaded, impossible to decapitate.[8] A swarm's behavior may look uncontrolled, even anarchic at times, but it is shaped by extensive consultation and coordination, made feasible by rapid communications among the parties to the swarm.[9]

The Zapatista case hints at the kind of doctrine and strategy that can make social netwar effective for transnational NGOs. Three key principles appear to be: (1) Make civil society the forefront—work to build a "global civil society," and link it to local NGOs. (2) Make "information" and "information operations" a key weapon—demand freedom of access and information,[10] capture media attention, and use all manner of information and communications technologies. Indeed, in a social netwar where a set of NGO activists challenge a government or another set of activists over a hot public issue, the battle tends to be largely about information—about who knows what, when, where, how, and why. (3) Make "swarming" a distinct objective, and capability, for trying to overwhelm a government or

---

[7]See Chapter Two for a discussion of network-based swarming. For further elaboration, see Arquilla and Ronfeldt (1997).

[8]However, particular leaders can make a difference. The development of many NGOs is at such an early stage that a leader's abilities and preferences can make a big difference as to how a specific NGO behaves. Brysk (1992) makes this point well and provides examples.

[9]Of course, there may be significant divisions and factions within a network that affect its overall shape and behavior. Intranetwars may arise that alter or limit the network's capacity.

[10]On efforts to create an international charter on NGOs' rights to information and communications, see Frederick (1993c), among other sources.

other target actor. Although, as noted above, swarming is a natural outcome of information-age, network-centric conflict, it should be a deliberately developed dimension of doctrine and strategy, not just a happenstance.

Where all this is feasible, netwarriors may be able to put strong pressure on state and market actors, without aspiring to seize power through violence and force of arms. In some instances, this may pose a potential threat to some U.S. interests. But in other cases, like Mexico's, a social netwar may amount to a challenge rather than a threat—it may even have some positive consequences, especially for spurring social and political reforms. Indeed, in its more positive aspects, the Zapatista netwar has not been bad for Mexico (or for U.S. interests), even though it has heightened uncertainty in Mexico and abroad regarding Mexico's stability and future prospects.

However, as discussed in Chapter Five, a recent development in the Zapatista case—a call for "electronic civil disobedience"—suggests that the theory and practice of social netwar could go in new directions. A split may even occur, akin to a traditional split on the Left between socialists and anarchists. To date, mainstream netwar activism has gone in the directions described above and elsewhere in this chapter: It has emphasized the creation of complex, multiorganizational networks, which use the new technologies mainly to improve communication and coordination within the network and to exert pressure on government and other actors through electronic protest measures (e.g., via e-mail and fax-writing campaigns). In contrast, a new "electronic civil disobedience" faction is emerging that appears to care less about the organizational network-creating dimensions of doctrine and strategy, favoring aggressive computer-hacking tactics that, though termed "virtual sit-ins," verge on anarchistic or even nihilistic "cybotage" against sensitive government or corporate Web sites and Internet servers.

FAVORABLE CONDITIONS FOR SOCIAL NETWAR

The Zapatista movement substantiates the growth of "global civil society" and has helped to catalyze it, showing it can reach from the global down to the local level and influence the policies of states. This netwar has affected not just Chiapas and Mexico; it is galvanizing a new presence in world politics that challenges the primacy of the nation-state in some issue areas.

The Zapatista case indicates some conditions that should be present for a transnational social netwar to emerge and spread. Evidently, as in the case of Mexico, a society should be relatively open (or opening up), including in regard to freedom of association and information. It should be in flux and under political, economic, and other strains that are generating divisive public debates. This may be especially the case in societies where old clannish and hierarchical structures are being challenged by, and adapting with difficulty to, new market and civil-society forces.[11]

The society should have local NGOs to which the transnational NGOs can link. The society should be in a region where the infrastructure for social activism is growing, in both organizational and technological terms. The activists should have diverse communication systems at their disposal for purposes of rapid all-channel consultation, coordination, and mobilization. The transnational NGOs and their networks should have sufficient reach that they can not only arouse public opinion, but also lobby in Washington and other capitals where policy decisions are made.

A target government should care about its international image, and be sensitive to its disruption.[12] The more a government cares about presenting to the world an image that it is, or is becoming, a modern democracy and wants to attract foreign investors, the more vulnerable it may be to a netwar that jeopardizes its image. A pariah state, like Iraq, that does not care much about its image in Washington or European capitals will be less vulnerable to social netwar, and less hesitant to crush activists who try to create one. (Perhaps a susceptibility to social netwar is a sign of modernity.)

Social netwar thrives on having audiences outside the conflict zone. Audiences should be aroused not only in the target society but also in distant, influential foreign capitals. Social netwar may be most effective where activists in a target society can appeal to strong, liberal, democratic audiences abroad whose own civil-society actors can

---

[11]For clarification and elaboration, see Appendix B.

[12]Sikkink (1993) addresses this point well.

take up the cause and lobby for changes in their government's policies toward the nation at issue. Getting the message from the conflict zone to such audiences abroad may be facilitated by the fact that this is the direction in which the Internet and other global media generally tend to convey information.

Indeed, a major part of social netwar is about activists' efforts to get their story into the global media, so that it reaches and arouses foreign publics and governments. Conditions should be such that a "CNN effect" can occur that amplifies the theatrical information operations of netwarriors. The local and international press should have access to and be captivated by the story. The mainstream press may not be part of a social netwar, in that it (usually) does not have an explicit agenda and does not form part of the NGO networks. Nonetheless, the presence of journalists may contribute importantly to a netwar by providing, very quickly, a broader audience than usual for NGO activities. A symbiotic dynamic may thus develop between the activists and the media (in which the journalists may claim that they are the ones who deserve credit for calling a conflict to the world's attention, but the larger dynamic is about the activists using the media to accomplish this). Furthermore, the media's presence may alter the local power equations vis-à-vis information—a local government may lose the luxury of controlling who knows what about a conflict, and its options may decrease accordingly. As international attention grows, a hard-line approach, for example, may be less feasible for a government.

Finally, the issues should be amenable to social activism. Some are easier than others for NGOs to take up. The more statecentric an issue area—the case, for example, with issues like military reform —the more difficult they may be for NGOs to address. Much may depend on whether there are international bodies concerned with the issues. As Brysk (1992) has observed, an indigenous people may face the following kinds of issues: being killed (a human-rights issue), poverty (a development issue), land theft (which becomes a migration issue), deforestation (an environmental issue), and land-use conflicts (which may be a market issue). In this situation,

> the rational response of a social movement is to launch simultaneous appeals in all appropriate venues—and over time, to concentrate on those issue areas governed by accessible and responsive

international regimes. In general, information-processing regimes such as human rights and ecology are more accessible to NGOs than state-centric arrangements for trade or arms control.[13]

In other words, the situation in a target society should be such that a diversity of NGOs exist and can mount different attacks on different issues, adapting flexibly to the circumstances. In the process, the message—the story and its symbolism—may get modified and broadened beyond its original meaning in the conflict zone, in order to appeal better to audiences abroad.

Because such conditions are not present everywhere—they apply less to Myanmar than to Mexico—some societies will provide more susceptible environments than others for social netwar. Where the conditions are ripe, the Mexican case implies that social netwar may put a liberalizing authoritarian regime on the defensive and, to some extent, spur new steps toward democratization. Moreover, some foreign capitals will provide more susceptible external targets than others for social netwar. The conditions identified above indicate that social netwar will be most effective where a conflict can be "exported" in order to arouse activists and policymakers in the capitals of a foreign power. This is much more likely to be the case with the United States than, for example, with a power like Japan, where transnational social activism is relatively weak and can even be ignored.

Thus, social netwar can be an agent of change that may have both positive and negative effects—it may represent "good news" as well as "bad news" for U.S. interests. Social netwar is also in its infancy as a mode of conflict; governments are just beginning to learn about it. Mexico is one of the first countries to experience it, but it is far from the last. The significance and effectiveness of social netwar are likely to grow around the world. In some cases, the United States may even want to foment one, or at least be positioned to benefit from its effects—or the United States may want to preempt a netwar that might start against a key ally (e.g., Saudi Arabia).

---

[13]Brysk (1992), p. 23. Also see Brysk (1998, forthcoming) for further discussion.

CHALLENGES TO AUTHORITARIAN SYSTEMS

A major proposition in the literature about the implications of the information revolution is that it compels closed systems to open up, and thus will prove damaging to totalitarian and authoritarian regimes. This proposition emerged particularly during the administration of President Ronald Reagan, when Secretary of State George Shultz, writing in 1985, before the revolutions of 1989 in Eastern Europe, forecast that

> the free flow of information is inherently compatible with our political system and values. The communist states, in contrast, fear this information revolution perhaps more than they fear Western military strength. . . . Totalitarian societies face a dilemma: either they try to stifle these technologies and thereby fall farther behind in the new industrial revolution, or else they permit these technologies and see their totalitarian control inevitably eroded. (Shultz, 1985, p. 716.)

If the Soviet regime adopted the new technologies, Shultz and others (e.g., Stonier, 1983) predicted that its leaders would have to liberalize their economic and political systems. Subsequent events in Eastern Europe, China, and to a lesser extent Latin America provided evidence for the democratizing effects of the information revolution. Since then, researchers (e.g., Builder and Bankes, 1990; Kedzie, 1995) have increasingly argued that the diffusion of the new technologies will speed the collapse of closed regimes and favor the rise of open ones.

One recent Pentagon-based analysis focuses on the Internet. According to Charles Swett (1995), authoritarian governments are threatened by the freedom of information that it represents:

> The Internet is the censor's biggest challenge and the tyrant's worst nightmare . . . Unbeknown to their governments, people in China, Iraq and Iran, among other countries, are freely communicating with people all over the world.

As a result, "Authoritarian countries are hesitating before allowing their people access to this technology," because the Internet poses a "significant long-term strategic threat to authoritarian regimes" which they will be ineffective in countering (Swett, 1995).

The other side of the picture is that guerrillas and other antiestablishment groups are making increasing use of the new communications technologies. While systematic evidence for this is lacking, anecdotal evidence abounds. According to one journalist, for example,

> Today, every group from the Irish Republican Army to Hamas and Peru's Shining Path has taken its struggles to the Internet, and in the process they have radically altered the nature of guerrilla action and civic protest around the world. Net surfers can now learn everything about the revolutionary struggles in Mexico and Peru, and even how to construct a pipe bomb. (Vincent, 1996.)

That authoritarian regimes are at a strong disadvantage is not a sure bet over the near term, however. Some such regimes—for example, China, Cuba, and Myanmar (Burma)—have managed to control access to the new technologies and to the Internet, without incurring high political or social costs at home or setbacks in foreign trade and investment. This does not disprove the proposition that the information revolution will eventually compel closed systems to become open, but it indicates that the process will be uneven, situational, and long term in perhaps many cases.

The Zapatista case generally substantiates these points, since it is partly a case of a liberalizing authoritarian regime being affected by activists using the Internet and other media. Our point, however, is not so much about the information *technology* revolution in general or the Internet per se. Our point is more about the organizational dimensions of the information revolution: Whether a netwar can topple a particular dictatorship will depend on the situation; but in general, many authoritarian regimes are likely to prove vulnerable to social netwar, viewed as a combined organizational, doctrinal, and technological phenomenon.

For example, the scenes of future social netwars could include such countries as Cuba, Nigeria, Russia, and Saudi Arabia. In Cuba, the prospects for social netwar are growing. Castro's government has begun to open the economy, but persists in political and social repression. Meanwhile, grass-roots groups, which are very few in number, are trying to open space for themselves inside Cuba and to connect to outside NGOs, including through faxes and e-mail

(Gonzalez and Ronfeldt, 1994; Press, 1996). Aspects of netwar have existed for decades in U.S.-Cuban relations, as in the U.S. broadcasting and Cuba's jamming of Television Martí and Radio Martí, as well as in the activities of pro- and anti-Castro groups in the United States. What could emerge before long are the conditions for a full-fledged social netwar, if Cuba becomes more open than is presently the case.

In Saudi Arabia, the ruling family keeps tight control, including through heavy surveillance and security measures. But an underground exists, and people's access to modern telecommunications is improving as a result of new connections to the Internet and plans for AT&T to upgrade the cellular telephone grid. Thus, opportunities may grow for an indigenous dissident movement to emerge and gain links to outside fundamentalist and even secular democratic forces. At the same time, the more Saudi Arabia's telecommunications systems become connected to the outside world, the higher the costs of repression and control may become for the ruling regime. Note, for example, that even a sleek information-age autocracy like Singapore's cannot prevent the rise of stealthy activists using faxes and e-mail (though so far they have not had much effect on weakening the regime there).

Even a country as closed as Myanmar (Burma) may be vulnerable to social netwar. "Free Burma" exile groups have organized into a network and have created an e-mail circuit and Web pages to promote the downfall of the military junta and support internal pro-democracy activists. With the motto, "When spiders unite, they can tie down a lion," the network has successfully pressured some foreign corporations to stop doing business there. According to one report, "the junta seems to be worried, despite the fact that nobody outside the government in Myanmar has access to the Internet."[13] To control dissidents, the junta has outlawed the unauthorized possession of computers that have networking capability as well as the use of computers to transmit information on such topics as state security, the economy, and national culture.[14]

---

[13]From "Arachnophilia," *The Economist,* August 10, 1996, p. 28.

[14]From a note taken from the *Financial Times,* October 5, 1996, as posted on the Internet. Also see Danitz and Strobel (1998, forthcoming).

Of course, authoritarian regimes will not respond lightly to the emergence of social netwars. In their efforts at counternetwar, they may try to monitor, harass, arrest, and expel both domestic and foreign activists; regulate the formation and behavior of NGOs through administrative and judicial methods; and even create "dummy" NGOs or GONGOs[15] to hijack an agenda. Furthermore, they may try to control the means of communication—by restricting access to the Internet, seizing unauthorized pieces of technology, pressuring journalists about what to report, or other measures. They may also try to provoke intranetwars by sowing dissent among the NGOs. And they may try to wage misinformation and disinformation campaigns to embarrass or confuse the netwarriors. Some, though certainly not all, of this is evident from the Mexican case.

Opposing authoritarian regimes in some nations may not be the only objective of netwarriors. In the years ahead, the possibility should not be overlooked that a major new global peace and disarmament movement may eventually arise from a grand alliance among diverse NGOs and other civil-society actors attuned to netwar.[16] They may increasingly have the organizational, doctrinal, technological, and social elements to oppose recalcitrant governments, as well as to operate in tandem with supranational organizations and national governments that may favor and support such a movement.

Social netwar is fundamentally antiestablishment. It may be used by leftists, or rightists, or anyone else with an antiestablishment agenda. It is more likely to be used against states, rather than by states.

---

[15]See page 35, footnote 16.

[16]This prediction, which appeared in the December 1996 draft of this study (and earlier in Arquilla and Ronfeldt, 1996b), has since come partially true, with the rise of the worldwide movement to ban land mines. Because of it, a social netwar has won a Nobel prize.

IMPLICATIONS FOR THE U.S. ARMY AND MILITARY STRATEGY[17]

Why should this matter to the U.S. Army? In large part, it matters because the world is changing in ways that may be more likely to present social netwars than traditional insurgencies in many nation-states that are allies of, or otherwise of interest to, the United States. By analyzing the Mexican case, we may better understand the patterns that may arise in other contexts, and the innovations that may become advisable for responding to them. Mexico provides a preliminary case study not only of social netwar, but also of some options for counternetwar.

This case confirms the major propositions about networks-versus-hierarchies posited in Chapter Two. The Zapatista networks have performed impressively against the Mexican hierarchies. The latter, in turn, have responded with interagency cooperation and tactical decentralization, as the emerging theory of netwar suggests. In addition, this case shows that information operations are an important, innovative aspect of information-age conflict. The fight over "information" has made the Zapatista conflict less violent than it might otherwise have been. But it has also made the conflict more public, disruptive, protracted, and difficult to isolate; it has had more generalized effects than if it had been contained as a localized insurgency. Thus, although the Mexican military has performed reasonably well militarily against the EZLN, has decentralized its organization, created new small units, improved its communications and mobility, and acquired new material and budgetary resources in the process, it has been bedeviled by many aspects of this new approach to conflict. The army in particular has seen its combat operations deterred and its image impugned to an unusual degree.

The Mexican case suggests that the U.S. Army should continue to improve its understanding of the growing roles of NGOs in environments affected by SSCs.[18] Is social netwar, where activist NGOs operate in tandem with an insurgent army, really a new phe-

---

[17]Many points in this and the next subsection are reiterated from previously published work by Arquilla and Ronfeldt (1996a, 1996b, 1997). For additional insights, see Berger (1998).

[18]RAND research by Jennifer Taw is inquiring into this matter in other cases.

nomenon? Or is it just more of the same, with a heavier emphasis on psychological operations and public relations? Does social netwar mean that a local military, not to mention the U.S. military as an ally, has to respond quite differently? Our study suggests that the answer to such questions is "yes," largely because of the protagonists' emphasis on information operations. More than likely, the local military (and the government) will find it needs to develop its own information strategies to deal with the NGOs.

Where feasible, it may be increasingly advisable to improve U.S. and allied skills for communication and even coordination with NGOs that can affect the course and conduct of a netwar. The Mexican case suggests that the U.S. Army may be increasingly called upon to provide "knowledge assistance" to allies for public and press relations, psychological operations, and the restructuring of command, control, communications, and intelligence (C3I) functions in response to netwars. Respect for human rights, and possibly for the looming matter of "information and communications rights," may play no small part in this.

Furthermore, this case indicates the importance of monitoring and analyzing what is transpiring in cyberspace, where information operations may be conducted out of much public sight. Some work (e.g., Swett, 1995) has been done on this, but much more is needed. As noted earlier, netwars are waged mainly in real life, but what occurs in the infosphere—particularly "on the Net"—may have significant bearing on the course and consequences of a conflict.[19] It took Mexican officials a while to realize the role of the Internet in the Zapatista netwar.

By conventional measures, the EZLN has never had much of an order of battle—just an odd mixture of weapons, and only a few sizable combat formations. Yet, by emphasizing information operations, it has done quite well. This accords with points made in another study (Arquilla and Ronfeldt, 1996a): A new generation of assessment methodologies may be needed, including to determine a protagonist's "information order of battle" and the intentions, capabilities, and vulnerabilities related to it—in short, for doing a new kind of net

---

[19]See page 11, footnote 6.

assessment. It may turn out that a new language and a new set of metrics must be devised. New centers and schools are already being established for the U.S. military to help address such challenges. The question might also be addressed as to what an "information war room" would look like.

As we in the United States grapple to define our own concepts of information, we should keep an eye on how they are being defined in other societies and cultures that are trying to take advantage of the information revolution. To some extent, the U.S. government should aim to identify operational concepts that may serve as the basis for alliances and other forms of cooperation, where relevant. But we should also enhance our knowledge of others in order to develop early warning of potential adversaries, including nonstate adversaries, who may invent information concepts that are unusually difficult for us to counter. This may be especially the case with psychological and cultural aspects of warfare.

CONCLUDING COMMENT

In sum, the Mexican case confirms, and portends, that netwars may be a natural next mode of conflict (and crime). The advent of netwar is a result of the rise of network forms of organization, which in turn is a result of the information revolution. Not all conflicts will involve netwar—many traditional modes of conflict and crime will persist—but netwar is already ascendant.

A few propositions (taken from Arquilla and Ronfeldt, 1996b) that we would reiterate in conclusion, all confirmed by the Mexican case, are as follows:

- Organization, and knowing how to organize, have always been a source of power, independently of the resources and skills available in an organization. Today, the network form is fast becoming a new source of power—as hierarchy has been for ages. It is especially a source of power for actors who previously had to operate in isolation from each other, and who could not or would not opt to coalesce into a hierarchical design where they would lose their independence and autonomy.

- Power is migrating to actors who are skilled at developing networks, and at operating in a world of networks. Actors positioned to take advantage of networking are being strengthened faster than are actors embedded in old hierarchical structures that constrain networking. This does not favor actors on any end of an ideological or political spectrum—it favors whoever can best master network design elements.

- At present, nonstate transnational actors appear to be ahead of government actors at using, and at being able to use, this form of organization and related doctrines and strategies. It takes skill to use them well, but the ease of entry and the deniability afforded by network designs imply an increasing "amateurization" of militant activism, terrorism, and crime (Hoffman, 1994). It is increasingly easy for protagonists to construct sprawling networks that have a high capacity for stealthy operations by individuals or groups, as well as for rapid swarming en masse.

Information—as a function of the technological and organizational innovations stemming from the information revolution—is now said to be a "force multiplier" (notably during the Gulf War, to the benefit of U.S. forces). Yet the more important point is that information, along with the attendant rise of the network form, is a "force modifier." Taking advantage of the information age is bound to require modifications in how forces are organized and deployed for offensive and defensive moves, perhaps especially where the objective is more about disruption than destruction.

More to the point, "information strategy" is emerging as a new tool of statecraft. U.S. officials are accustomed to emphasizing economic, political, and military strategies and instruments for urging foreign governments and societies to develop in liberal democratic directions. Yet, global civil-society NGOs whose focus is informational more than economic, political, or military may prove more potent as information-age instruments of policy and strategy, especially to pursue goals like "democratic enlargement." Chris Kedzie's (1995) work on the positive correlation between political democracy and communications connectivity provides a basis for proposing that information be treated and developed as a distinct new dimension of policy and strategy (see Arquilla and Ronfeldt, 1996a, 1997, and forthcoming).

Understanding the network form is important for understanding the advent of netwar—why and how the world is giving rise to a new mode of conflict. More research lies ahead to improve our ability to study this form, its levels of analysis (e.g., the organizational, doctrinal, technological, and social levels), and its emerging implications for society and security in the information age. Better theories and methodologies are needed on how networks function and how best to analyze them. The age—and the study—of networks and netwars is barely beginning.

CHRONOLOGY OF THE ZAPATISTA SOCIAL NETWAR
(1994–1996)

January 1994. The EZLN launches an attack and occupies four municipalities. The movement declares war on the Mexican army, solicits the intervention of other powers, and calls for the resignation of the President and the establishment of a temporary government.

President Salinas quickly sends in 12,000 troops, and after two battles with the EZLN, the rebels retreat into the jungle. The army follows and launches attacks in armored vehicles, supported by air strikes. By January 12, with public and international opinion strongly against the fighting, Salinas declares a unilateral cease-fire and calls on the Zapatistas to lay down their arms and negotiate with the newly formed Commission for Peace and Reconciliation.

February–March 1994. Peace talks begin February 21 in San Cristóbal de las Casas in the town cathedral and under the aegis of Bishop Samuel Ruíz, with former Mexico City Mayor Manuel Camacho Solís representing the Mexican government. The site is guarded by concentric rings of the Mexican military police, civilian volunteers from the Mexican Red Cross, and a dozen national and local NGOs.

This chronology focuses on the 1994–1996 period, because that corresponds to the heyday of the Zapatista social netwar. The chronology was compiled as background material for this study mainly in mid-1996; it has been briefly updated for this publication. Various sources were used. A good, handy guide is the weekly *Mexico Update* that is prepared by Equipo Pueblo, a Mexican human-rights NGO, and posted on the Internet. A good guide to the Mexican government's view appears in a publication by the Consulado General de Mexico (Los Angeles), "Chiapas: Hechos y Realidades," January 1998.

The Zapatistas begin the talks with representatives from four Mayan-language groups, and they raise thirty-four issues pertaining to political, economic, and social reform. Two weeks later, the negotiators announce agreement on thirty-two tentative accords, and the talks recess with the Zapatistas returning to consult with their indigenous "constituents."

On March 22, PRI presidential candidate Luis Donaldo Colosio is assassinated in Tijuana one day after chief negotiator Camacho ends rumors and declares that he will not run an independent campaign for president. Public debate about the Zapatistas and the government is polarized in response to the violence. With the confusion and infighting within the PRI, the EZLN fears an attack by the army.

June 1994. In communal assemblies, the Zapatista rank and file reject the tentative peace accord negotiated by their representatives. Marcos declares that 98 percent of the *indigenas* voted against acceptance of the government proposals, with 3 percent voting to continue the war, and 97 percent favoring continuing dialogue. The EZLN calls for a national convention to reform the national political system and refuses to lay down arms. Further, it recognizes in "The Second Declaration of the Lacandón Jungle" that violence is not the only route to democracy, and calls upon civil society to lead the social change. Zedillo characterizes the earlier negotiations as a failure and blames Camacho, who resigns as the government's representative.

August 1994. The leadership of the EZLN, the CCRI-General Command, convenes civil society for a "National Democratic Convention" inside rebel territory. The goals of the convention are to prepare for the "defense of the popular will" should the PRI win the upcoming elections, and to draft a new Mexican constitution. The convention is modeled on the October 1914 "Revolutionary Sovereign Convention" of Emiliano Zapata in Aguascalientes, which attempted to establish a unified revolutionary government. A communiqué from Marcos establishes that "those who think armed struggle" is the only way to end PRI dominance, and those "who are not willing" to try the electoral path are "NOT convoked" to the convention.

Six thousand delegates attend, including representatives from many parts of civil society, and the cultural and social elite of Mexico and Latin America. After convening the convention, the EZLN withdraws, declaring that the movement will obey the convention's dictates, whatever they may be. Five work groups are created which ultimately urge participation in the upcoming August 21 elections and an active and massive public defense of the ballots afterward.

On August 21, 1994, Zedillo wins the presidential election for the PRI by a large margin. Many observers declare widespread fraud in balloting, although the *New York Times* declares the elections "the cleanest in memory." In Zapatista-held territory, the ballots show 70 percent of the 19,000 votes cast going to Cárdenas. Nationally, 77 percent of the eligible electorate votes, compared to the typical figure of less than 50 percent.

December 1994. Tensions rise in Chiapas as the military, with 20,000 troops in the state, surrounds EZLN forces in the eastern jungle, leaving only the Guatemalan border as an escape route. Since October 10 the Zapatistas had broken off contact with the government and the military had displayed a willingness to maintain a low profile and avoid further accusations of human-rights violations.

On December 8, the PRI's gubernatorial candidate is sworn in as Chiapas' governor, in spite of protests of widespread fraud.

On December 19, Marcos announces that the EZLN has broken out of the Army's cordon and taken 38 municipalities. Although untrue, the claim provokes economic panic, with investors selling sufficient stocks and bonds to force the devaluation of the peso.

January 1995. The Zapatistas declare an end to offensive military operations in anticipation of a new round of talks. Marcos meets with the new Minister of the Interior and both agree to renew a truce. The EZLN demands, and the government accepts, that the military withdraw from rebel territory it had recently occupied and that Bishop Ruíz be allowed to resume mediation. Negotiations begin for restarting the peace talks. As PRD demonstrators protest in Tabasco and peasants seize a town hall in Chiapas, the government agrees to hold new elections in both states.

February 1995. Zedillo announces on February 10 that the EZLN has refused to respond to government overtures and that the government has uncovered the identity of the movement's top leaders, including Marcos. He orders the military to assist in their arrest. The army quickly moves into the jungle, encountering little resistance. Many Zapatistas are arrested in army and police raids in Mexico City, Veracruz, and Chiapas. Captured leaders include "Vicente," "Eliza," and "Santiago."

The government comes under attack from all quarters for its offensive, with protesters taking to the streets, U.S. human-rights activists and members of congress urging Clinton to pressure Mexico, and the PRI suffering huge electoral defeats in elections in Jalisco and Guadalajara. On February 14, Zedillo orders the military to halt offensive action, cancels the arrest warrants against top EZLN leaders, and makes a new appeal for dialogue. The new governor of Chiapas is forced to step down, meeting a key Zapatista demand. The government and EZLN agree to meet formally in April to negotiate a time and place for peace talks.

March 1995. For the first time in Mexico's history, the president and the legislative branch agree to promote a bill which will be submitted to the Mexican congress. The bill—the Law for Dialogue and Reconciliation and a Dignified Peace in Chiapas—calls for the creation of the necessary conditions for a dialogue and negotiations, foresees the adoption of commitments for a peace agreement, and attempts to meet the underlying causes of the conflict. One of its major provisions is amnesty for EZLN members. After initially rejecting the bill, the Zapatistas indicate their willingness to resume dialogues.

April 1995. After several days' delay, the government and EZLN open several days of talks in Chiapas on April 22. The dialogue is meant to establish the process for establishing a détente and the protocol for later peace negotiations.

May 1995. EZLN negotiators accept the government's proposal for a "Program of Integrated, Progressive, Reciprocal, Proportional, and Verifiable Détente." They pledge to take the issue before their rank and file for consultations. The meeting represents the first direct peace talks between the EZLN and Zedillo.

June 1995. Zapatista leaders indicate that their rank and file, after consultations, reject entirely the government's proposal for détente. On June 7, the third round of negotiations begins, and one day later, both parties agree on the ground rules for future talks. The Zapatistas call for a "national consultation" where civil society will join together in the fight for democracy.

July 1995. Two further rounds of talks occur in Chiapas, but without any agreements on the two major themes of security corridors for the EZLN and procedural rules for peace talks.

August 1995. The EZLN conducts a national "referendum" on its political future, establishing polling booths in many parts of Mexico, including Mexico City, on August 27. Of Mexico's 40 million eligible voters, slightly more than one million participate in the referendum. Fifty-three percent believe that the EZLN should become an independent political force (with 38 percent voting no), while 48 percent vote for it to join other political organizations (and 44 percent vote no).

September 1995. Phase six of the peace talks begins on September 6, using a new negotiation procedure to speed them up. On the 11th, the government and the Zapatistas finally agree on the procedures to regulate the talks, a subject that had been discussed since April. The topics for discussion will be Indigenous Rights and Culture, Social Welfare and Development, and Justice and Democracy.

October 1995. Local elections in Chiapas are held without incident during phase seven of the peace talks, which establish the format for the negotiations on Indigenous Rights and Culture. Elections are canceled in a few municipalities because of an "air of tension" and an indigena refusal to nominate candidates or permit the presence of election officials in several locations. Results show the PRI winning in most municipalities.

In the middle of negotiations on Indian rights, the Mexican government arrests top Zapatista leader "Germán" in Mexico City. The government claims that the arrest is not in violation of the amnesty agreement made in April because his arrest was not based on his EZLN ties, but rather for possession of weapons and one gram of cocaine. "Germán" denies any involvement with the movement. The EZLN issues a "red alert," charges the army with aggressive troop movements, and disappears further into the jungle to discuss whether to continue with the negotiations. One week later, the charges against "Germán" are dismissed at the request of the Attorney General's Office.

November 1995. A federal judge acquits "Commander Eliza" of sedition and weapons charges after her February arrest, setting the basis for the release of 18 other alleged Zapatistas arrested at the same time.

On the 17th the government and EZLN reach a preliminary 25-point agreement on Indian rights and culture in the first substantive phase of the negotiations.

January 1996. The Zapatistas issue their "Fourth Lacandón Jungle Declaration," in which civil society is invited to take part in a new national political force, to be called the Zapatista National Liberation Front (FZLN). The front will be based on EZLN ideals and will stand as a broad opposition movement and a place for citizen political action. The EZLN dedicates "Aguascalientes II," four new cultural centers in Chiapas that were constructed during December. On January 10 the third Indian rights and culture talks (and the tenth overall meeting) convene between the government and the Zapatistas. Topics of discussion include the autonomy of Indian groups, greater political participation for indigenous people in legislative organizations, and the creation of autonomous zones. Both parties agree to establish a new social pact and new relationship among the state, society, and indigenous people, and also to acknowledge in the constitution Indians' political, social, cultural, jurisdictional, and economic rights, as well as their autonomy.

February 1996. The congress of Chiapas commits itself to promoting 22 reforms of the local constitution and civil, penal, and electoral codes, and to modify the basic law of the judicial branch in order to consolidate the political, economic, social, and cultural rights of the state's indigenous people. The EZLN and the government sign the first peace accords, after 11 months of negotiations. A major point in the agreements recognizes indigenous people in the constitution.

March 1996. Talks begin on reforms for the state of Chiapas. The government states that it only wants to discuss local issues and that the EZLN is not relevant to the discussion. The Zapatistas accuse the government of returning to its attitude of April–July 1995.

April 1996. EZLN and government advisors meet for a round of talks on "democracy and justice," representing phase two of the second point on the negotiation's agenda. The government accuses the Zapatistas of using delaying tactics in order to organize a national forum on the subject.

May 1996. Alleged EZLN member Javier Elorriaga Verdegue is sentenced to 13 years in prison, having been found guilty of membership in the EZLN, terrorism, conspiracy, and rebellion. Elorriaga asserts that he is the victim of a political trial and that he had only been a go-between for the government and the EZLN leadership. In response, the EZLN indicates that it will reconsider participation in the peace talks until the release of Elorriaga and another alleged Zapatista, Sebastian Etzin Gomez. Many NGOs begin mobilizing to demand their release.

As a consequence of the convictions and other tensions, the talks reach their most critical juncture since April 1995, with talk of postponing or canceling the June 5 round of negotiations.

June 1996. The EZLN accepts the proposal of the National Mediation Commission (CONAI) to postpone the June 5 talks between the government and Zapatistas, thus preventing a breakoff of the negotiations. The movement indicates a willingness to continue with the peace process, but only if the government meets a number of conditions, including the release of Elorriaga and Etzin and an end to military mobilization. EZLN advisor Antonio Garcia de Leon alleges that in the past fifteen months 60,000 troops have massed in Chiapas and that the government is increasing its counterinsurgency actions with "massive imports" of equipment for use against "drug trafficking" and advancing in a "slipknot" operation from at least seven garrisons in Chiapas.

On June 6, Elorriaga and Etzin are released after no criminal evidence is brought against them. Within hours they both declare themselves Zapatistas. Their release decreases the tensions in the state.

On June 11, the EZLN and the government agree to discuss a new legal framework and format for the peace talks to avoid "constant shifts and tension." The Zapatistas end their "maximum alert" and Marcos notes that the movement prefers talks, but "not at any cost."

The Popular Revolutionary Army (EPR) makes its presence known in Guerrero, and proceeds to carry out a series of coordinated armed actions in various states, mainly during July and August.

July 1996. The government and the EZLN appear to arrive at an agreement about how to resume their negotiations, including about the composition of the Commission for Follow-Up and Verification of the Peace Accords, whose creation had been delayed since February.

The first "Intercontinental Encounter for Humanity and against Neoliberalism" is convened by the EZLN, in Oventic, Chiapas. It attracts thousands of foreign activists and various global media.

August 1996. Peace talks resume in San Andres, but quickly stalemate.

September 1996. The EZLN announces an indefinite suspension of its participation in the dialogue at San Andres, pending the formation of a better government negotiating team, the release of alleged Zapatista prisoners, and compliance with the January 1996 agreement on indigenous cultural rights, among other things.

Marcos sends a public letter to the EPR stating that the EZLN and the EPR are fighting for different objectives and that the EZLN does not want or need the EPR's support.

RETHINKING MEXICO'S STABILITY AND TRANSFORMABILITY

Assessing the potential for stability or instability in Mexico has always been something of a guessing game, in which prominent, skillful guessers often turn out to be wrong. Consider the period of the early and middle 1980s, when Mexico seemed "on the brink" of collapse (Castañeda, 1986) because of "multiple crises" (Latell, 1986) and the threat of a spillover of revolutionary trends in Central America. Yet, while many Mexicans suffered from economic hardships in this period, there were no major episodes of unrest; the system did not collapse, and its leaders successfully initiated some major economic reforms. Although there are many reasons why the forecasts of collapse proved wrong, an important one was not noticed until later: the strength and dependability of the extended family system in Mexico, which provided a widespread informal social net for members who had economic troubles and needed assistance and even sheltering for awhile.

Consider another period—the late 1980s and early 1990s—when many analysts argued that Mexico's economic liberalization policies and the advent of NAFTA would, or should, result in more progress and stability than ever before. But this has been dispelled by the EZLN and the EPR; the economic crisis of 1994 is said to have been

---

This section was drafted independently by David Ronfeldt, and it does not necessarily implicate the other authors of this study. This section was once part of the main text, but it raised so many comments that it seemed advisable to either remove it entirely or relegate it to an appendix. The latter option was chosen. Only a few concluding paragraphs from this appendix remain in the text.

worse than the one in 1982. Mexico's stability seemed suddenly in doubt. There are many reasons why the preceding forecasts no longer look good. But again, an important factor was neglected or underplayed: corruption and criminality. Experts on Mexico, be they Mexicans or Americans, normally give a nod to corruption, and maybe also to criminality, in their analyses of the Mexican system. But none have given this factor the weight that recent events indicate it deserves. Indeed, the dynamics of the Mexican system now appear to depend as much on it as on the strength of the PRI and the presidency. This dark factor even helps explain why Mexico's economic liberalization and privatization policies, among other things, have not had as many widespread beneficial results as academic analysts expected.

Against this background, this author is wary of trying to provide a blanket or a nuanced bottom-line, single-point assessment of the prospects for stability or instability in Mexico. Instead, some tentative ideas are posed for thinking about those prospects in a somewhat new way. The outlook is medium to long term, and it rests on some broad dynamics. It may not satisfy readers who are looking for a standard assessment of current conditions and trends—e.g., an assessment that would examine the status of President Zedillo and his policies, of the PRI and its possible decline as a political force, of the relationships between economic and political trends, of the growing role of the military, etc. But it does offer the reader a "long view"[1] of some types of instability and of some scenarios that Mexico (and the United States) may have to face in the years ahead.

THREE TYPES OF INSTABILITY—AND FOUR SCENARIOS

Instability comes in many shapes and sizes. What one analyst means by the term may not be the same for another. For example, each may have a different threshold in mind, such that what qualifies as instability for one analyst may not for another—and they end up talking past each other.

Here, an effort is made to distinguish among three types—in a sense, a scale—of instability:

---

[1] Term taken from Schwartz (1991).

- Sporadic instability—in which outbreaks of unrest occur, often as a reaction to current conditions and trends, but the unrest remains relatively isolated, and isolatable, so that it does not jeopardize the political system as a whole. A better term than "sporadic" should be found, but the point remains: Here I am referring to disturbances and other manifestations of instability—say a labor strike, a student demonstration, even a provincial insurgency—that have local dimensions, depend on very specific demands, and do not stress the response capabilities of the government or its security forces.

- Systemic instability—in which unrest diffuses and shakes the foundations of the ruling institutions, so that a collapse, a constitutional or succession crisis, a palace revolution, a military coup, or some other highly irregular disruption occurs (e.g., a "dark alliance" between gangsters and guerrillas that gravely undermines the state) or is likely to occur. This is what is usually meant by the term "instability."

- Evolutionary instability—in which a society cannot make the change to a new system that has higher evolutionary potential, for example, by changing from an authoritarian statist regime to a market-oriented democratic regime. The society hardens around the existing stage, gets stuck in the transition process, or falls apart under the strain, perhaps resulting in a great social revolution. This term also does not sound quite right, and a better one may yet be found.[2] Meanwhile, it is a major reason for posing this tripartite distinction. Of the three, it may well be the major issue for Mexico in the years ahead—and the key issue may be whether Mexico can successfully adapt to the market system. This needs explaining, which is done below in the discussion about the "TIMN framework."

These terms appear to refer to different degrees of instability—and in a sense, they do. But more is at work than just degrees. Each step in-

---

[2]This type of instability includes what other writers may view as revolutionary instability—the society is so unstable that a full-scale social revolution seems likely, as happened before in Mexico, Russia, China, and Cuba. The view presented here—which will become clearer in the discussion of the TIMN framework—is that there is a deeper dynamic at work, namely an incapacity for evolutionary transformation, and a new social revolution is only one of several possible effects.

volves somewhat different dynamics. It is not simply a sliding or cumulative scale. For example, a Mexico affected by "evolutionary" instability is not necessarily fraught with "systemic" and "sporadic" instability. Indeed, it is possible that the existing Mexican system is quite stable and that the key problems are the other two types, especially the evolutionary type. The scale also hints at the point that a lot of sporadic instability may mean something is wrong with the system as a whole, yet the system is not necessarily unstable or must/will be changed. Sporadic instability, if properly handled, may help to spur reforms and relieve pressures that might lead to worse instability. Curiously, however, a lot of sporadic instability can be used to frame an argument that Mexico is too unstable to risk further reform—this has not been uncommon in Mexico's recent history.

Four scenarios about Mexico's future seem reasonable to present that relate, in various ways, to these distinctions:[3]

- Major instability—in which, because of massive violent unrest, elite infighting, or other reasons, the political and economic systems break down, with dire consequences. This scenario could be the result of a mix of all three types of instability posited above.

- Criminalization—in which drug traffickers and other criminal mafias gain so much power and influence, including through the use of paramilitary and quasi-guerrilla forces, that a variant of "Colombianization" takes hold. In this scenario, powerful clannish, family-based mafias that are already embedded in Mexico's system take advantage of all types of instability, and perhaps foment some, in order to strengthen their hold (and their holdings). Mexico is characterized by criminal mercantilism, and possibly strategic crime against the United States. Reports about Mexican crime families taking over the command-and-control functions once dominated by the Colombian drug-trafficking cartels help substantiate this scenario.

- A "stuck system"—in which Mexico's leaders, operating in ever-shifting alliances, make halting advances with political and eco-

---

[3]I am indebted to a discussion with Brian Jenkins in which these four scenarios were first spelled out.

nomic reforms, but traditional, deeply embedded nationalist and corporatist principles continue to be reasserted, prompting periodic slowdowns, reversals, and distortions in the reform process. Mexico's decision to halt and revise its plans to privatize the petrochemical sector helps substantiate this scenario. Mexico does not quite cross the threshold to having a truly democratic, market-oriented system—and many elites are contented with that. In this scenario, to reiterate an old aphorism, the more the system changes, the more it remains the same—and keeps returning to remain the same. Evolutionary instability is a key issue here; but the scenario also implies continued levels of sporadic instability.

- Successful transformation—in which Mexico's leaders succeed in implementing a range of political, economic, and other reforms, and Mexico muddles through, or breaks through, to build a truly democratic, market-oriented system. In this scenario, sporadic instability may still occur, especially in provincial areas; but it helps spur Mexico's rulers to implement needed reforms. Systemic instability becomes moot, and Mexico transcends the prospect of evolutionary instability.

There is nothing unusual about the two polar scenarios—the ones about major instability, and successful reform. Versions of them often appear in scenario layouts about the future of Mexico. One might even say they are tantamount to "vanilla" scenarios, in that versions of them appear in most layouts about most countries—there is little that is inherently and uniquely Mexican about them. What look more interesting are the other two scenarios—the ones about criminalization and the "stuck system." They reflect historic and continuing realities in Mexico; they are genuinely Mexican scenarios.

It is premature to rank order the relative likelihood of the three types of instability, or of the four scenarios. But what they help show is that the prospects for evolutionary instability, and for the "stuck system," look pretty high and deserving of further attention. The next section outlines a theoretical argument that is meant to add to an understanding of this.

PRELIMINARY APPLICATION OF THE TIMN FRAMEWORK TO MEXICO[4]

What forms account for the organization and evolution of societies? How have people organized their societies across the ages? The answer may be reduced to four basic "forms" of organization:

- the kinship-based *tribe*, as denoted by the structure of extended families, clans, and other lineage systems;

- the hierarchical *institution*, as exemplified by the army, the (Catholic) church, and ultimately the bureaucratic state;

- the competitive-exchange *market*, as symbolized by merchants and traders responding to forces of supply and demand;

- the collaborative *network*, as found today in the web-like ties among some NGOs devoted to social service and advocacy.

Each of these four basic forms, writ large, represents a distinctive system of values, beliefs, structures, and dynamics about how a society should be organized—about who gets to achieve what, why, and how. Each form has enabled people to do something better—to address and solve some problem that societies are bound to face—than they could by using another form. Each form attracts and engages different types of actors and adherents.

Incipient versions of all four forms were present in ancient times. But as deliberate, formal organizational designs with philosophical portent, each has gained strength at a different rate and matured in a different historical epoch over the past 5,000 years (partly because, in order to mature, each form requires a new revolution in the information and communications technologies of the time). Tribes developed first, hierarchical institutions next, and competitive markets later. Now, collaborative networks appear to be on the rise as the next great form of organization to achieve maturity.

---

[4]Explication of the TIMN framework appears in Ronfeldt (1996); a shorter version is in Arquilla and Ronfeldt (1996b). Early thoughts about its application to Mexico appear in Ronfeldt and Thorup (1995) and Ronfeldt (1995). Much work must still be done to develop the framework.

The nature of each form is briefly discussed below, in this case with relevance to Mexico, as a prelude to pointing out that they can be assembled in a framework—currently called the "TIMN framework"—about the long-range evolution of societies. The persistent argument is that these four forms—and evidently only these[5] —underlie the organization of all societies, Mexico included, and that the historical evolution and increasing complexity of societies has been a function of the ability to use and combine these four forms of governance. Although the tribal form initially ruled the overall organization of societies, over time it has come to define particularly the cultural realm. Meanwhile, the state has become the key realm of institutional principles, and the economy of market principles. Civil society seems to be the realm most affected and strengthened by the rise of the network form, auguring a vast new rebalancing of relations among state, market, and civil-society actors around the world.

In the case of Mexico, all four forms, and the mentalities that pertain to each of them, are in play. Mexico's prospects for stability, for responsible, effective government, and for economic and political transformation depend on which forms and which combinations prevail.

The first form that any successful society is built on is the tribal, which dates from primitive eras. Its essential principle is kinship, be it of blood or brotherhood. A basic result is the definition of a society's bedrock culture, including its ethnic and linguistic traditions.

At its best, this form enables a society to have a sense of social identity and belonging. It fosters egalitarian behavior toward other members of the clan or tribe. In modern eras, it lays the basis for nationalism. Mexico has this (though it also has numerous *indigenas* who have yet to rise above a local ethnicity). Indeed, Mexico's stability and progress since the 1910 Revolution have depended on the tribe-like solidarity of the "revolutionary family" of ruling elites. Mexico's bedrock culture also benefits, as noted earlier, from the durability of the extended family system.

---

[5]Class, which many social scientists regard as a basic form of organization, is, in this framework, not a basic form but a result of interactions among and experiences with the four basic forms.

At its worst, this form fosters a narrow-minded clannishness that arrogantly justifies anything to protect, enrich, and strengthen a clan, its leaders, and their fiefdoms. Then it thrives on nepotism and favoritism, and may lead to vengeful, murderous feuds. This dark side may be found among political gangsters, crime lords, and *caciques* in Mexico. It may lie partly behind some assassinations.

The second form, which arose under the ancient empires and later the absolutist states of the 16th century, is institutional. Its essential principle is hierarchy, and it enables a society to advance by developing a powerful center for decision, control, and coordination—a center that is absent in the classic tribe. The key result is a strong state that is sensitive about issues of sovereignty.

At its best, this form leads to professional, authoritative institutions to govern a nation. Mexico has progressed in this respect. For decades, the PRI-government system, despite its faults, has given Mexico a strong state based on corporatist and clientelist structures. Today, Mexico is in the process of trying to develop a new generation of well-educated, honest, responsible administrators.

At its worst, this form undergirds the rise of corrupt, arbitrary, dynastic (even tribal) hierarchies that covet power, operate in secrecy, and prefer impunity to the law. This fits the worst descriptions of the traditional PRI and government pyramids, the "old guards" of political "dinosaurs" and provincial *caciques*, and the structures of some state enterprises and labor unions.

The third form, which developed rapidly in the 18th century on the eve of the Industrial Revolution, is that of the market. Its essential principle is open competition among private interests that behave freely and fairly. Its strength is that it enables a society to process complex transactions better than the first two forms can. And its key result is a market system that operates independently of the state.

At its best, this leads to a productive, diversified, innovative economy. In Mexico, this form has had difficulty taking root since the last century, partly because of strong resistance from the prior two forms, which prefer collectivism and statism respectively. But the economic restructurings that were initiated by Presidents de la Madrid and Salinas de Gortari and are now being deepened by President Ernesto Zedillo represent solid, promising, and probably irreversible gains.

But this form also has a dark side. It can allow for unbridled, unproductive, short-term speculation, and it can lead to the rigging of protected market sectors for the benefit of minorities of powerful, wealthy capitalists and special interests, some of whom may indulge in rapacious exploitation. This still exists in Mexico's quasi-market system.

The fourth form, the latest to mature around the world, is that of the information-age network (what might be called the "cybernet" form). Its key principle is mutual consultation and collaboration among members of a distributed, multiorganizational network. While this form has existed for ages, it is now able to mature because of the increasing availability of new information technologies—advanced telephones, fax machines, e-mail, computer billboards and conferencing systems—that can enable small, autonomous, dispersed groups to coordinate and act jointly across great distances. As shown by the global growth of environmental, peace, human-rights, and advocacy networks, and by the increasing resort of health, education, and welfare organizations to networked designs, this form is gaining strength particularly among social actors. The key result in the decades ahead will probably be the strengthening of civil-society actors relative to state and market actors at local, national, and global levels. Either that, or a new sector or realm may emerge for which there is no name yet.

At its best, this form seems likely to result in vast networks of NGOs to address social equity and accountability issues that the other forms do not address well. This positive side of this form has begun to take hold in Mexico, notably through the rise of human-rights and pro-democracy NGOs.

But this form can have a dark side too: It can strengthen "uncivil society," for example by enabling subversive groups to conduct campaigns of public deception and disinformation, by helping guerrilla groups to coordinate widespread attacks, or by undergirding transnational criminal organizations that develop networks in Mexico to smuggle drugs, arms, or migrants, or to launder money.

In Mexico—and elsewhere—more is at stake, and in conflict, than just the bright versus the dark sides of these four forms. Even the bright sides are in conflict. For example, in the south, the Zapatista *indigenas* have egalitarian ideals that reflect classic tribal patterns of behavior. They prefer slow communal consultations to fast decisionmaking by impersonal state institutions. Moreover, in the name of "community," these ideals prefer to reject "the market." (Indeed, very strong clan and tribal dynamics tend to limit a people's ability to develop sound institutional and market systems.) In Mexico's center and north, tensions exist between, on the one hand, proponents of the statist form, who prevail in traditional, left-leaning intellectual and political circles, and on the other hand, proponents of the market form, who are found in business-related circles. And of course, the rise of pro-market and pro-network forces, especially those that have transnational ties, poses a challenge to the statist defenders of Mexico's traditional views of national sovereignty. But contradictions and tensions between the adherents of each form are only part of the story.

Ultimately, what matters for a society is how the forms get added together, and how well they function together for the society as a whole. In historical terms, a society's advance has depended on its ability to use and combine the forms in a natural progression. Over the ages, societies organized in tribal (T) terms are surpassed by societies that also develop institutional (I) systems to become T+I societies, often with strong states. In turn, these get superseded by societies that allow space for the market form (M), and become T+I+M societies. Now the network (N) form is on the rise, with special relevance for civil society. We are entering a new phase of evolution in which T+I+M+N societies will emerge to take the lead. To do well in the 21st century, an information-age society must incorporate all four forms—and they must function well together despite their inherent contradictions.

Every society, and Mexico is no exception, must move at its own pace and develop its own approach to each form and their combinations, in a process that requires modifying the older forms to adapt to the newer. In historical terms, it is often difficult—and it takes decades or longer—for a society to adapt to each form and relate it to those that developed earlier. Indeed, the values, norms, and "spaces" favored by one form tend to contradict those favored by another. Moreover, the rise of a new form can induce systemwide transformations and epochal philosophical and ideological struggles. This explains some of the social turbulence in the United States, which has begun the transition to a T+I+M+N society. It also helps explain the volatility of Mexico, which is moving haltingly to develop a T+I+M system at a time, on the eve of the 21st century, and in a neighborhood, North America, that is rife with the growth of +N forces and their spillover effects.

Success is not inevitable. A society may get stuck, go astray, or be torn apart as it tries to adapt to a new form. Indeed, the great social revolutions of the 20th century—the Mexican, as well as the Russian, Chinese, and Cuban revolutions—all occurred in T+I societies where old clannish and hierarchical structures were under stress from flawed infusions of capitalist market practices. Failing to make the transition to become T+I+M societies, they reverted to T+I regimes that, in all but Mexico's case, transformed absolutism into totalitarianism. Today, to varying degrees, these nations are trying anew to make the same transition. Mexico appears to stand the best chance of succeeding, especially if it does not get stuck.

Mexico has had a statist, largely undemocratic T+I system most of this century, and the forces that prefer to maintain it that way remain strong, even fierce, at national and local levels, especially among old guard elements of the PRI and PRD parties in central and southern Mexico. Although capitalism has made inroads for decades, this has not meant that an open market system was being developed. Mexico did not begin moving effectively to become a T+I+M system until the 1980s. It has not completed the transition, and the actors who want this advance in the complexity, versatility, and adaptability of the Mexican system still seem to be a minority. Even the recent privatization of many state enterprises, whose effectiveness is crucial for building a solid market system, has been conducted in a clannish manner involving favoritism.

For the Mexican system, then, the key evolutionary challenge at this stage is to adopt and adapt to the market system and integrate it into society as a whole. The reasons are cultural and political as much as economic. If Mexico cannot convert to a T+I+M society, then the open competitive principles that the market form ideally represents will not take root and spread throughout the social system—Mexico will remain a mostly T+I society that chronically exhibits the rhetoric but not the reality of democracy. For the +M transition to be fully realized, the government must continue distancing itself from the

PRI, and the party system must become more openly and fairly competitive in the wake of the marketization of the economy.

Many trends and events that have recently disturbed Mexico—such as the conflict in Chiapas, the apparent infighting between traditional and modernizing forces in PRI and government circles, the rising influence of drug traffickers, the periodic disarray in financial matters, the growing denunciations of neoliberalism, the uneasiness among investors, the growing disparities between the northern and southern regions, the rise of new civil-society actors—all reflect, directly or indirectly, (a) the difficulties Mexico is having accepting the market form and its principles of openness and competition, and (b) the unsettling feedback effects that this form's rise has on the old, defensive clannish and hierarchical structures, as well as (c) the complexity of making the +M transition when +N forces are also gaining strength and having complex, ambivalent effects. Mexicans are gradually making room for the market form in the nation's overall design, but progress has been erratic, even among business elites, and it has aroused some strong, even violent resistance.

TENTATIVE IMPLICATIONS FOR STABILITY AND REFORM

Thus, what will prevail is still up in the air: Continued progress toward a democratic T+I+M system (that also has +N elements)? Reversion to a neocorporatist T+I system? Or something else that may bring authoritarian solutions, and a new set of problems?

A complete reversion is surely beyond the pale. Many economic and political reforms since the 1980s seem irreversible. But a resurgence of negative opinions—e.g., that Mexico is not suited to marketization, that statist designs are better for Mexico, that national identity, dignity, and sovereignty are weakened by liberalization, that Mexico's system cannot withstand more instability, and that the "colossus to the north" is interested only in exploitation—indicate that exponents of both the bright and dark sides of the T and I forms may yet keep the M from flowering. Thus, while a complete reversion to the old T+I system may not be possible, archaic forces could constrain the achievement of a positive +M combination and of a broadly democratic system. In other words, Mexico could get stuck.

The effort to make a transition from one evolutionary stage to the next is bound to generate social contradictions and conflicts, as all sectors try to adjust to new forces and new realities. Mexico's halting transition from a T+I to a T+I+M system is causing, and will go on causing, all sorts of minor and some major disturbances. At times, this may mean labor union strikes, or electoral protests, or shootouts involving drug traffickers and other criminals, or protest demonstrations by students, environmental or human-rights activists, or creditors (as in the *Barzón* movement), etc. At times, the scene may be a major city; often it may be a provincial area where *caciquismo* is entrenched. Sometimes, a conflict will take the form of a netwar, but traditional forms of conflict will also arise and endure. The list of possibilities is long and diverse.

At the moment, Mexico's governing institutions appear to be strong enough that such disturbances should prove manageable, challenging but not jeopardizing Mexico's systemic stability. Indeed, the serious risk for Mexico is not an old-fashioned civil war or another revolution—that seems unlikely. The greater risk is a plethora of social, guerrilla, and criminal netwars. Mexico's security in the information age may be increasingly a function of netwars of all varieties. Mexico already appears to be the scene of more types of divisive, stressful netwars than other societies at a similar level of development, in part because it is a neighbor of the United States.

At present, neither social (EZLN/Zapatista), guerrilla (EPR), or criminal (drug-trafficking) netwar actors seem likely to make Mexico ungovernable, or to create a situation that leads to a newly authoritarian regime. This *might* occur, if these netwars all got interlaced and reinforced each other, directly or indirectly, under conditions where an economic recession deepens, the federal government and the PRI (presumably still in power) lose legitimacy to an alarming degree, and infighting puts the elite "revolutionary family" and its political clans into chaos. All this seems quite unlikely, however, since in many respects Mexico seems in better shape now than in the early and middle 1980s, when many analysts argued that breakdown or collapse might be imminent. However, an eye should be kept on the period just before, during, and after the year 2000 elections. Could this provide a propitious time for an old guard *Priista* with criminal bearings to gain his party's presidential nomination? For guerrilla groups like the EPR to take to the field? For a subtle interplay to be developed between gangster and guerrilla groups that allows for the imposition of a heavy-handed regime whose darker purposes include strategic crime and criminal mercantilism?

The challenge may not be so much safeguarding the governability of Mexico as coping with the netwars and other disturbances in ways that assure both the continued stability and transformability of the Mexican system. Both dynamics, stability and transformability, are at stake; and there is no easy relationship between them—sometimes stability can be enhanced by economic and political reforms, at other times it can be disturbed by such reforms. There is a risk that Mexico will remain stable but, in the process, will succumb to the criminalization scenario or see its capacity for transformation become so confounded and constrained that the "stuck system" scenario prevails.

BIBLIOGRAPHY

Acosta, Mariclaire, "Democracy, Governability, and Human Rights in Mexico," *Enfoque*, Spring/Summer 1997, pp. 1, 10, 12, 14, 16.

Arizpe, Lourdes, "Chiapas: The Basic Problems," *Identities: Global Studies in Culture and Power*, Vol. 3, No. 1–2, October 1996, pp. 219–233.

Arquilla, John, and David Ronfeldt, "Cyberwar Is Coming!" *Comparative Strategy*, Vol. 12, No. 2, Summer 1993, pp. 141–165. Available as RAND reprint RP-223.

—— and ——, "Information, Power, and Grand Strategy: In Athena's Camp," in Stuart J.D. Schwartzstein (ed.), *The Information Revolution and National Security: Dimensions and Directions*, Washington, D.C.: Center for International and Strategic Studies, 1996a, pp. 132–180.

—— and ——, *The Advent of Netwar*, Santa Monica, CA: RAND, MR-789-OSD, 1996b.

—— and —— (eds.), *In Athena's Camp: Preparing for Conflict in the Information Age*, Santa Monica, CA: RAND, MR-880-OSD/RC, 1997.

—— and ——, *The Emergence of Noopolitik: Toward an American Information Strategy*, Santa Monica, CA: RAND, MR-1033-OSD, forthcoming.

————, ————, and Michele Zanini, "Information-Age Terrorism and the U.S. Air Force," in Ian O. Lesser et al., *Countering the New Terrorism*, Santa Monica, CA: RAND, MR-989-AF, forthcoming.

Asprey, Robert, *War in the Shadows*, New York: Morrow, 1994.

Bailey, John, and Sergio Aguayo (eds.), *Strategy and Security in U.S.-Mexican Relations Beyond the Cold War*, San Diego: Center for U.S.-Mexican Studies, University of California at San Diego, 1996.

Barry, Tom (ed.), *Mexico: A Country Guide*, The Inter-Hemispheric Education Resource Center, Albuquerque, NM, 1992.

Beam, Louis, "Leaderless Resistance," *The Seditionist*, Issue 12, February 1992 (text can also be located sometimes on the Internet).

Berger, Alexander, "Organizational Innovation and Redesign in the Information Age: The Drug War, Netwar, and Other Low-End Conflict," master's thesis, Monterey, CA: Naval Postgraduate School, 1998.

Brysk, Alison, "Acting Globally: International Relations and Indian Rights in Latin America," paper presented at the XVII International Congress of the Latin American Studies Association, Los Angeles, September 24–27, 1992.

————, "Acting Globally: Indian Rights and International Politics in Latin America," in Donna Lee Van Cott (ed.), *Indigenous Peoples and Democracy in Latin America*, New York: St. Martin's Press, 1994.

————, "Turning Weakness Into Strength: The Internationalization of Indian Rights," *Latin American Perspectives*, Vol. 23, No. 2, Spring 1996, pp. 38–57.

————, *From Tribal Village to Global Village: International Relations and Indian Rights in Latin America*, Stanford, CA: Stanford University Press, 1998 forthcoming.

Builder, Carl H., and Steven C. Bankes, *The Etiology of European Change*, Santa Monica, CA: RAND, P-7693, December 1990.

Builta, Jeffrey A., "Harakat al-Muqawama al-Islamiya (Hamas)," in John Murray and Richard H. Ward (eds.), *Extremist Groups*, Chicago: University of Illinois Press, 1996, pp. 775–794.

Burguete Cal y Mayor, Araceli, "Maya Identity and the Zapatista Uprising," *Abya Yala News*, Vol. 8, No. 1 and 2, Summer 1995, pp. 6–11.

Camp, Roderic Ai, "Militarizing Mexico: Where Is the Officer Corps Going," unpublished research draft, January 1997.

Campen, Alan, Douglas Dearth, and R.T. Goodden (eds.), *Cyberwar: Security, Strategy and Conflict in the Information Age*, Fairfax, VA: AFCEA International Press, 1996.

Carr, Barry, "From the Mountains of the Southeast: A Review of Recent Writings on the Zapatistas of Chiapas," *Journal of Iberian and Latin American Studies*, Vol. 13, No. 2, December 1997 (as posted on the Internet).

Castañeda, Jorge G., "Mexico at the Brink," *Foreign Affairs*, Winter 1986, pp. 287–303.

———, "Chiapas and the National Crisis," *Hemisphere*, Vol. 6, No. 1, Winter/Spring 1994, pp. 34–35.

———, *The Mexican Shock: Its Meaning for the United States*, New York: The New Press, 1995.

Castells, Manuel, *The Power of Identity* (The Information Age: Economy, Society and Culture, Volume II), Malden, MA: Blackwell Publishers, 1997.

Castro Soto, Oscar, "Elementos Para un Analisis de Coyuntura y una Posible Estrategia desde las Clases Populares y las Organizacionses no Gubernamentales," in Mario B. Monroy (ed.), *Pensar Chiapas, Repensar México: Reflexiones de las ONGs Mexicanas*, Mexico: Convergecia de Organismos Civiles por la Democracia, August 1994.

Cleaver, Harry, "The Chiapas Uprising and the Future of Class Struggle in the New World Order," for *RIFF-RAFF*, Padova, Italy,

February 1994a (online at gopher://lanic.utexas.edu:70/11/la/ Mexico/).

———, "Introduction," in Editorial Collective, *¡Zapatistas! Documents of the New Mexican Revolution*, Brooklyn: Autonomedia, 1994b (online at gopher://lanic.utexas.edu:70/11/la/Mexico/ Zapatistas/).

———, Posting to Chiapas-L list on the Internet, March 20, 1995a.

———, Edited reposting to Chiapas-L list on the Internet, March 20, 1995b.

———, "The Zapatistas and the Electronic Fabric of Struggle," draft, November 1995c (posted at http://www.eco.utexas.edu/faculty/ Cleaver/zaps.html), for publication in John Holloway (ed.), *The Chiapas Uprising and the Future of Revolution in the Twenty-First Century*, in preparation.

———, "The Zapatista Effect: The Internet and the Rise of an Alternative Political Fabric," *Journal of International Affairs*, Vol. 51, No. 2, Spring 1998, pp. 621–640.

———, "The Zapatistas and the International Circulation of Struggles," draft conference paper, February 1998 (as circulated on the Internet).

Collier, George, "Roots of the Rebellion in Chiapas," *Cultural Survival Quarterly*, Vol. 18, No. 1, Spring 1994a, pp. 14–18.

———, with Elizabeth Lowery Quaratiello, *BASTA! Land and the Zapatista Rebellion in Chiapas*, A Food First Book, Oakland, CA: Institute for Food and Development Policy, 1994b.

Danitz, Tiffany, and Warren P. Strobel, *Networking Dissent: Burmese Cyberactivists Promote Nonviolent Struggle Using the Internet*, Washington, D.C.: U.S. Institute for Peace, 1998 forthcoming.

Davis, Diane E., "Failed Democratic Reform in Mexico: From Social Movements to the State and Back Again," *Journal of Latin American Studies*, Vol. 26, No. 2, May 1994, pp. 375–408.

Dawkins, Richard, *The Selfish Gene*, New York: Oxford University Press, 1989.

Diaz del Castillo, Bernal, *The Conquest of New Spain* [1568], Baltimore: Penguin, 1963.

Diaz-Polanco, Hector, "Autonomy for Mexico's Indigenous Peoples," *Enfoque*, Spring/Summer 1997, pp. 3, 4, 9, 17.

Dresser, Denise, "Treading Lightly and Without a Stick: International Actors and the Promotion of Democracy in Mexico," 1994, published in Tom Farer (ed.), *Beyond Sovereignty: Collectively Defending Democracy in the Americas*, Baltimore, MD: Johns Hopkins University Press, 1996, pp. 316–341.

Estrada Martínez, Rosa Isabel, and Gisela Gonzalez Guerra (eds.), *Tradiciones y Costumbres Jurídicas en Comunidades Indigenas de México*, Mexico City: Comisión Nacional de Derechos Humanos, 1995.

Evan, William M., "An Organization-Set Model of Interorganizational Relations," in Matthew Tuite, Roger Chisholm, and Michael Radnor (eds.), *Interorganizational Decisionmaking*, Chicago: Aldine Publishing Company, 1972, pp. 181–200.

Fox, Jonathan, "The Difficult Transition from Clientelism to Citizenship: Lessons from Mexico," *World Politics*, Vol. 46, No. 2, January 1994, pp. 151–184.

——— and Luis Hernandez, "Mexico's Difficult Democracy: Grassroots Movements, NGOs and Local Government," *Alternatives*, Vol. 17, 1992, pp. 165–208.

Frederick, Howard, "Computer Networks and the Emergence of Global Civil Society," in Linda Harasim (ed.), *Global Networks: Computers and International Communication*, Cambridge, MA: MIT Press, 1993a, pp. 283–295.

———, *North America NGO Networking on Trade and Immigration: Computer Communications in Cross-Border Coalition-Building*, Santa Monica, CA: RAND, DRU-234-FF, 1993b.

———, *Global Communication and International Relations*, Belmont, CA: Wadsworth Publishing Co., 1993c.

Fuentes, Carlos, "Chiapas: Latin America's First Post-Communist Rebellion," *New Perspectives Quarterly*, Vol. 11, No. 2, Spring 1994, pp. 54–58.

Fuller, Graham, "The Next Ideology," *Foreign Policy*, No. 98, Spring 1995, pp. 145–158.

Furniss, Edgar, *DeGaulle and the French Army*, New York: The Twentieth Century Fund, 1964.

Gann, Lewis, *Guerrillas in History*, Stanford, CA: Hoover Institute, 1971.

Gelernter, David, *Mirror Worlds, or the Day Software Puts the Universe in a Shoebox . . . How It Will Happen and What It Will Mean*, New York: Oxford University Press, 1991.

Gerlach, Luther P., "Protest Movements and the Construction of Risk," in B. B. Johnson and V. T. Covello (eds.), *The Social and Cultural Construction of Risk*, Boston: D. Reidel, 1987, pp. 103–145.

——— and Virginia Hine, *People, Power, Change: Movements of Social Transformation*, New York: The Bobbs-Merrill Co., 1970.

Gonzalez, Edward, and David Ronfeldt, *Storm Warnings for Cuba*, Santa Monica, CA: RAND, MR-452-OSD, 1994.

Gonzalez Casanova, Pablo, "Causes of the Rebellion in Chiapas," *Identities: Global Studies in Culture and Power*, Vol. 3, No. 1–2, October 1996, pp. 269–290.

Goss, Adrienne, with Jared Smith, "NGOs and the Global Community," March 29, 1995 (as posted on the Internet).

Gossen, Gary H., "Comments on the Zapatista Movement," *Cultural Survival Quarterly*, Vol. 18, No. 1, Spring 1994, pp. 19–21.

Gray, Chris Hables, *Postmodern War: the New Politics of Conflict*, New York: The Guildford Press, 1997.

Griffith, Samuel, *Mao Tse-Tung on Guerrilla Warfare*, New York: Praeger, 1961.

Group 2828, "Net, Which Net? Or, Our Collective Hammock. Or, the Net, which represents us all. Or, collectively we are stronger!" 1997 (as posted on the Internet at http://www.eco.utexas.edu/ homepages/faculty/Cleaver/wk1net.html).

Guevara, Che, *Guerrilla Warfare* [1960], Lincoln: University of Nebraska Press, 1985. Translated by J.P. Morray.

Guillermoprieto, Alma, "The Shadow War," *New York Review*, March 2, 1995, pp. 34–43.

Harvey, Neil, "Rebellion in Chiapas: Rural Reforms, Campesino Radicalism, and the Limits to Salinismo," *Transformation of Rural Mexico*, Number 5, Ejido Research Project, La Jolla, CA: Center for U.S.-Mexican Studies, 1994, pp. 1–43.

Hellman, Judith Adler, *Mexico in Crisis*, 2d ed., New York: Homes and Meier, 1988.

Henissart, Paul, *Wolves in the City: The Death of French Algeria*, New York: Simon and Schuster, 1970.

Hernandez, Luis, "The Chiapas Uprising," *Transformation of Rural Mexico*, Number 5, Ejido Research Project, La Jolla, CA: Center for U.S.-Mexican Studies, 1994a, pp. 44–56.

———, "The New Mayan War," *NACLA: Report on the Americas*, Vol. 27, No. 5, March/April 1994b, pp. 6–10.

Hernandez, Ricardo, and Edith Sanchez (eds.), *Cross-Border Links: A Directory of Organizations in Canada, Mexico, and the United States*, Albuquerque, NM: The Inter-Hemispheric Education Resource Center, 1992.

Hoffman, Bruce, *Responding to Terrorism Across the Technological Spectrum*, Santa Monica, CA: RAND, P-7874, 1994.

Kedzie, Chris, "Democracy and Network Interconnectivity," Proceedings of INET '95, Honolulu, June 1995.

Kelly, Kevin, *Out of Control: The Rise of Neo-Biological Civilization*, New York: A William Patrick Book, Addison-Wesley Publishing Company, 1994.

Kelly, Ross, *Special Operations and National Purpose*, Toronto: Lexington Books, 1989.

Latell, Brian, *Mexico at the Crossroads: The Many Crises of the Political System*, The Hoover Institution, Essays in Public Policy No. 6, Stanford University, Stanford, CA, June 16, 1986.

Le Bot, Yvon, *Subcomandante Marcos: El Sueño Zapatista*, Mexico City: Plaza & Janés, 1997.

Lenin, V.I., "On Guerrilla Warfare" [1916], *Orbis*, Vol. 2, Summer 1958, pp. 194–208.

Lipschutz, Ronnie D., "Reconstructing World Politics: The Emergence of Global Civil Society," *Millennium: Journal of International Studies*, Winter 1992, pp. 389–420.

Lynch, Aaron, *Thought Contagion: How Belief Spreads Through Society*, New York: Basic Books, 1996.

Mahon, John K., *History of the Second Seminole War*, Gainesville, FL: University of Florida Press, 1992.

Manheim, Jarol, *Strategic Public Diplomacy and American Foreign Policy: The Evolution of Influence*, New York: Oxford University Press, 1994.

Mathews, Jessica, "Power Shift," *Foreign Affairs*, Vol. 76, No. 1, January/February 1997, pp. 50–66.

Maurer, Eugenio, "Autoridad, Comunidad Y Armonia En El Mundo Tseltal," in Rosa Isabel Estrada Martínez and Gisela Gonzalez Guerra (eds.), *Tradiciones y Costumbres Jurídicas en Comunidades Indigenas de México*, Mexico City: Comisión Nacional de Derechos Humanos, 1995.

Meisel, James, *The Fall of the Republic: Military Revolt in France*, Ann Arbor: University of Michigan Press, 1962.

Molander, Roger C., Andrew S. Riddile, and Peter A. Wilson, *Strategic Information Warfare: A New Face of War*, Santa Monica, CA: RAND, MR-661-OSD, 1996.

Monroy, Mario B. (ed.), *Pensar Chiapas, Repensar México: Reflexiones de las ONGs Mexicanas*, Mexico: Convergecia de Organismos Civiles por la Democracia, August 1994.

Nash, June, "The Reassertion of Indigenous Identity: Mayan Responses to State Intervention in Chiapas," *Latin American Research Review,* Vol. 30, No. 3, 1995, pp. 7–41.

Nugent, Daniel, "Northern Intellectuals and the EZLN," *Monthly Review*, Vol. 47, No. 3, July–August 1995 (as circulated on the Internet).

Nye, Joseph S., *Bound to Lead: The Changing Nature of American Power*, New York: Basic Books, 1990.

———— and William A. Owens, "America's Information Edge," *Foreign Affairs*, Vol. 75, No. 2, March/April 1996, pp. 20–36.

O'Donnell, Susan, and Guillermo Delgado P., "Using the Internet to Strengthen the Indigenous Nations of the Americas," *Journal of Media Development*, March 1995 (as posted on the Internet, December 20, 1995).

Orozco Zuarth, Marco A., *Sintesis de Chiapas*, Mexico City: Ediciones y Sistemas Especiales, 1995.

Paret, Peter, *French Revolutionary Warfare from Indochina to Algeria*, New York: Praeger, 1964.

Pazos, Luis, *Porque Chiapas?* Mexico City: Editorial Diana, 1994.

Prescott, W.H., *A History of the Conquest of Mexico* [1843], New York: Heritage, 1949.

Press, Larry, "Cuban Telecommunications, Computer Networking, and U.S. Policy Implications," Santa Monica, CA: RAND, DRU-1330-1-OSD, 1996.

Preston, Shelley, "Electronic Global Networking and the NGO Movement: The 1992 Rio Summit and Beyond, "*Swords and Ploughshares: A Chronicle of International Affairs*, Vol. 3, No. 2, Spring 1992 (as posted on the Internet).

Radu, Michael, "Mexican and Peruvian Answers to Marxist Insurgencies, 1980–1997: A Comparative Analysis," draft, DIA Contract # MDA 90897 M 7302, September 25, 1997.

Reding, Andrew, "Chiapas Is Mexico: The Imperative of Political Reform," *World Policy Journal*, Vol. 11, No. 1, Spring 1994, pp. 11–25.

Reygadas Robles Gil, Rafael, "Espacio Civil por la Paz," in Mario B. Monroy (ed.), *Pensar Chiapas, Repensar México: Reflexiones de las ONGs Mexicanas*, Mexico: Convergecia de Organismos Civiles por la Democracia, August 1994.

Rifkin, Jeremy, *The End of Work: The Decline of the Global Labor Force and the Dawn of the Post-Market Era*, New York: G. P. Putnam's Sons, 1995.

Ronfeldt, David (ed.), *The Modern Mexican Military: A Reassessment*, Monograph Series, #15, Center for U.S.-Mexican Studies, University of California at San Diego, 1984.

———, "Cyberocracy Is Coming," *The Information Society*, Vol. 8, No. 4, 1992, pp. 243–296. Available as RAND reprint RP-222.

———, "Institutions, Markets, and Networks: A Framework About the Evolution of Societies," Santa Monica, CA: RAND, DRU-590-FF, December 1993.

———, "Batallas mexicanas en Internet," *NEXOS*, #216, Diciembre 1995, pp. 47–51.

———, *Tribes, Institutions, Markets, Networks: A Framework About Societal Evolution*, Santa Monica, CA: RAND, P-7967, 1996.

——— and Armando Martínez, "A Comment on the Zapatista Netwar," 1996, in Spanish translation in Sergio Aguayo and John Bailey (coords.), *Las Seguridades de Mexico y Estados Unidos en un Momento de Transicion*, Mexico City: Siglo XXI, 1997, pp. 320–346.

——— and Peter Reuter, *Quest for Integrity: The Mexican-U.S. Drug Issue in the 1980s*, Santa Monica, CA: RAND, N-3266, 1992. (Excerpts published in the *Journal of Interamerican Studies and World Affairs*, Fall 1992, pp. 89–153.)

———— and Cathryn Thorup, *North America in the Era of Citizen Networks: State, Society, and Security,* Santa Monica, CA: RAND, P-7945, 1995. Edited version, in Spanish translation in Sergio Aguayo and John Bailey (coords.), *Las Seguridades de Mexico y Estados Unidos en un Momento de Transicion,* Mexico City: Siglo XXI, 1997, pp. 271–319.

————, ————, Sergio Aguayo, and Howard Frederick, "Restructuring Civil Society Across North America in the Information Age: New Networks for Immigration Advocacy Organizations," Santa Monica, CA: RAND, DRU-599-FF, 1993.

Ross, John, *Rebellion from the Roots: Indian Uprising in Chiapas,* Monroe, ME: Common Courage Press, 1995.

Schwartz, Peter, *The Art of the Long View: Planning for the Future in an Uncertain World,* New York: Currency Doubleday, 1991.

Schulz, Donald, *Mexico and the Future,* Carlisle Barracks, PA: U.S. Army War College, Strategic Studies Institute, September 25, 1995.

Scott, David C., "NGOs Achieve Credibility in Mexico," *Crosslines Global Report,* October 31, 1995 (as posted on the Internet).

Shultz, George, "New Realities and New Ways of Thinking," *Foreign Affairs,* Spring 1985, pp. 705–721.

Shy, John, and Thomas W. Collier, "Revolutionary War," in Peter Paret (ed.), *Makers of Modern Strategy,* Princeton: Princeton University Press, 1986, pp. 815–862.

Sikkink, Kathryn, "Human Rights, Principled Issue-Networks, and Sovereignty in Latin America," *International Organization,* Vol. 47, No. 3, Summer 1993, pp. 411–442.

Simon, Joel, "Netwar Could Make Mexico Ungovernable," Pacific News Service, March 13, 1995.

Slaughter, Anne-Marie, "The New World Order," *Foreign Affairs,* Vol. 76, No. 5, September/October 1997, pp. 183–197.

Spiro, Peter J., "New Global Communities: Nongovernmental Organizations in International Decision-Making Institutions," *The Washington Quarterly,* Vol. 18, No. 1, Winter 1995, pp. 45–56.

Stephen, Lynn, "Democracy for Whom? Women's Grassroots Political Activism in the 1990s, Mexico City and Chiapas," in Gerardo Otero (ed.), *Neo-Liberalism Revisited: Economic Restructuring and Mexico's Political Future*, Boulder, CO: Westview Press, 1996.

Stephens, John Lloyd, *Incidents of Travel in Central America, Chiapas and Yucatan* [1841], New York/London: Harper/Century, 1988.

Sterling, Claire, *Thieves' World: The Threat of the New Global Network of Organized Crime*, New York: Simon and Schuster, 1994.

Stern, Kenneth, *A Force upon the Plain: The American Militia Movement and the Politics of Hate*, New York: Simon and Schuster, 1996.

Stonier, Tom, "The Microelectronic Revolution, Soviet Political Structure, and The Future of East/West Relations," *Political Quarterly*, April–June 1983, pp. 137–151.

Swett, Charles, *Strategic Assessment: The Internet*, Washington, D.C.: Office of the Assistant Secretary of Defense for Special Operations and Low-Intensity Conflict (Policy Planning), The Pentagon, July 17, 1995 (as posted on the Internet by the Project on Government Secrecy of the Federation of American Scientists).

Szafranski, Colonel Richard, "Neo-Cortical Warfare? The Acme of Skill," *Military Review*, November 1994, pp. 41–55.

———, "A Theory of Information Warfare: Preparing for 2020," *Airpower Journal*, Spring 1995, pp. 56–65.

Taber, Robert, *The War of the Flea*, New York: Citadel, 1970.

Tello Díaz, Carlos, *La Rebelión de las Cañadas*, Mexico City: Cal y Arena, 1995.

Thomas, Hugh, *Conquest: Montezuma, Cortes, and the Fall of Old Mexico*, New York: Simon and Schuster, 1993.

Thorup, Cathryn L. "Politics of Free Trade and the Dynamics of Cross-Border Coalitions in U.S.-Mexican Relations," *Columbia Journal of World Business*, Vol. 26, No. 2, Summer 1991, pp. 12–26.

————, "Building Community Through Participation: The Role of Non-Governmental Actors in the Summit of the Americas," in Robin Rosenberg and Steven Stein (eds.), *Advancing the Miami Process: Civil Society and the Summit of the Americas*, Coral Gables, FL: North-South Center Press, 1995, pp. xiii–xxvi.

Toffler, Alvin, and Heidi Toffler, *War and Anti-War: Survival at the Dawn of the Twenty-First Century*, Boston: Little, Brown and Company, 1993.

Trejo Delarbreed, Raul (ed.), *Chiapas: La Guerra de las Ideas*, Mexico City: Editorial Diana, 1994, including selected articles by Luis Hernandez Navarro, Javier Gill, Xschitl Leyva Solano, Gaston Garcia Cantu.

Urry, Ruth Nikola, "Rebels, Technology, and Mass Communications: A Comparative Analysis of FMLN and EZLN Media Strategies," master's thesis, Department of Latin American Studies, Tulane University, March 1997.

Van Cott, Donna Lee, *Defiant Again: Indigenous Peoples and Latin American Security*, McNair Paper 53, Washington, D.C.: Institute for National Strategic Studies, October 1996.

Van Creveld, Martin, *The Transformation of War*, New York: Free Press, 1991.

Villafuerte Solis, Daniel, and Maria del Carmen Garcia Aguilar, "Los Altos de Chiapas en el Contexto del Neoliberalismo: Causas y Razones del Conflicto Indigena," in Silvia Soriano Hernandez (ed.), *A Proposito de la Insurgencia en Chiapas*, Mexico City: Asocacion para el Desarrollo de la Investigacion Cientifica y Humanistica en Chiapas, 1994.

Vincent, Isabel, "Rebel Dispatches Find Home on Net," *The Globe and Mail* (Toronto), June 11, 1996, p. A1 (as posted on the Internet).

Wager, Stephen J., "Chiapas y las Relaciones entre Civiles y Militares," *Este País*, Abril 1995, pp. 12–17.

———— and Donald Schulz, "The Awakening: The Zapatista Revolt and Its Implications for Civil-Military Relations and the Future of

Mexico," *Journal of Interamerican Studies and World Affairs*, Vol. 37, No. 1, Spring 1995, pp. 1–42.

Waldrop, M. Mitchell, *Complexity: The Emerging Science at the Edge of Order and Chaos*, Simon & Schuster, New York, 1992.

Wehling, Jason, "'Netwars' and Activists Power on the Internet," March 25, 1995 (as circulated on the Internet in the abridged version, "'Netwars': Politics and the Internet," August 7, 1995. The full version is posted at http://www.teleport.com/~jwehling/ OtherNetwars.html).

Whaley, Patti, "Potential Contributions of Information Technologies to Human Rights," keynote speech to Canadian-U.S. Human Rights Information Documentation (CUSHRID) Conference, November 4–5, 1995 (as posted on the Internet).

Williams, Phil, "Transnational Criminal Organizations and International Security," *Survival*, Vol. 36, No. 1, Spring 1994, pp. 96–113.

Womack, John, "La Revuelta Zapatista," *Nexos*, No. 237, Septiembre 1997, pp. 39–47.

Wray, Stefan, "Looking for Ideas on Networks in Encuentro Documents," July 1997 (as posted on the Internet).

———, "On Electronic Civil Disobedience," paper presented to the 1998 Socialist Scholars Conference Panel on Electronic Civil Disobedience, March 1998a (as posted on the Internet).

———, "Transforming Luddite Resistance into Virtual Luddite Resistance: An Earth First! Cyber-Manifesto," draft, April 2, 1998b, prepared for publication in the *Earth First! Journal* (as posted on the Internet). (This draft was only temporarily available on the Internet; it was evidently edited for publication and replaced by a shorter version, dated April 7, 1998. The April 2 version is preferred for this study.)